MARSTON GREEN

From olden days to the present day

*Dedicated to the staff of Marston Green Library, Elaine Allen
and Helen Flannery, for many months of assistance and
friendly advice extended to me whilst producing this book.*

*Local section taken off Warwickshire Tapestry in Warwick Museum.
Commissioned in 1580 to Ralph Sheldon. (1537/1613)*

MARSTON GREEN

From olden days to the present day

GRAHAM E CRAWFORD

BREWIN BOOKS

First published by
Brewin Books Ltd, 56 Alcester Road,
Studley, Warwickshire B80 7LG in 2010
www.brewinbooks.com

ISBN: 978-1-85858-463-8

A Cataloguing in Publication Record
for this title is available from the British Library.

Typeset in Palatino
Printed in Great Britain by
Hobbs the Printers Ltd.

TABLE OF CONTENTS

Chapter 1

INTRODUCTION

I CAME TO Marston Green as a 2 year old having been born in Hobmoor Road, Small Heath in 1926, but obviously not having any say or knowledge of the move at that age. My father, Edmund Crawford, was a grocer working for his father, but wishing to move on he became the Manager of 'Wrensons' grocery shop in Station Road, Marston Green, (nowadays 'Flair' Door Centre).

Shortly after, in 1930, we moved again as my father wished to start on his own, he took over the 'Chelmsley Drug Store' in Holly Lane, which was an early Pharmacy shop owned by a Mrs. Louisa Bates. She apparently had decided to retire, due to another Pharmacy being opened in Station Road in the same position as present day, with Ronald Campbell as the owner.

My father then opened under his own name as a Grocer and Greengrocer with the premises being extensively enlarged and with new living accommodation being added above the old building.

I started school in 1931 in the old timber classrooms situated where the Clinic and Library are now located. The classrooms were cold in winter months and we used to get a bottle of milk (before Margaret Thatcher stopped it) which was heated by a small coke burning stove which stood in the corner of each classroom. Mr. Clarence ('gaffer') Bates was the Headmaster, Miss Peel taught the Infants, and whilst I was there two new teachers arrived, Frank Cooper and Miss Banks, (later Mrs. Mary Walker). Both of them stayed at the school until their retirements.

In 1937 I moved on to Coleshill Grammar School when it was positioned at the top of Church Hill, adjacent to the Coleshill Parish Church. In those days it catered for boys only. Many boys from Marston Green attended the Grammar School and most of us made the journey by bicycle by way of Coleshill Road and Coleshill Heath Road. There were no school buses in those days, and the normal bus service started from the city terminus at the 'Bull Ring' in Birmingham in front of 'St.Martin's Church' travelled down the Coventry Road, turned off to Sheldon, into Marston Green and on to Coleshill. If my memory is correct, I believe there was only one bus which ran every two hours to Coleshill, and then returned to Birmingham.

In summer months we often returned home by leaving Coleshill via an old track, (which is now Green Lane) then across the fields to the Chester Road, entered into

'Chelmsley Woods' past 'Alcott Hall Farm' and finally up Wood Lane to Chelmsley Lane and into the village.

I joined in most of the village activities available for youngsters in those days, Boy Scouts with Wilf Martin and Peter Arton as the Leaders. There were 'Ropeholders' at the Free Church and a Youth Club at the Village Hall with a Mr. Whitehouse as Leader, he cycled from Sheldon in the war years as the bus rarely ran when bombing occurred. I joined the 'Heart of England Air Training Corps' based at Coleshill and I remember Malcolm Keen was in charge and he lived in Coleshill Road.

I left school in 1942 and started work at 'Metropolitan Cammell' who were making 'Valentine Tanks' at that time. They had a visit from General Bernard Montgomery and he gave us his rallying cry of "Give us the tools and we will finish the job" speech.

In January 1945 I joined the Royal Navy. By the time I had finished my training the war had ended. I spent 2 years overseas based mainly at Hong Kong and had spells on 2 ships, H.M.S. 'Trafalgar' a Battle Class Destroyer and a Light Fleet Carrier H.M.S. 'Glory'. I have always been active in sport and played soccer, cricket and hockey whilst in the Royal Navy. In January 1948 I returned to civvy street and my former employers.

When I returned home I played cricket and soccer for Marston Green teams, and was a member of Marston Green Golf Club for some 15 years when it was an 18 hole course. 'Anno domini' brought an end to soccer and cricket but I still play golf (badly) at Maxstoke Park Golf Club.

I married my wife Joan (Clarke) in 1955, and since then we have lived in Elmdon Lane and Coleshill Road, and in 2005 to the present address in Bickenhill Road. We had 3 daughters, Jeanette, Gillian and Kathryn and since then 4 grand daughters Emily, Hannah, Victoria and Eleanor. Sadly, my wife passed away in 2007 despite a long and courageous battle against a terminal illness.

Having previously written an earlier book, I have since obtained much more significant information and details about Marston Green in days gone by. I do now realise that some of the statements in the earlier book do need correcting and in some cases can be improved in the light of fresh information that was not available first time round.

Further to this, details which were certainly correct some 12 years ago, are simply not applicable or correct today, particularly in respect of shops and traders that have changed, or sadly disappeared from the village. I have attempted to up date all of this wherever possible.

So here we go again!

Chapter 2

FOREWORD

PRIOR TO the 40th Anniversary of the Marston Green Library I was asked to supply copies of my earlier book 'Domesday to Millennium'. Secondly, whilst looking at the excellent display presented by the Library staff, some incorrect information and claims were on display submitted by other contributors which I believe should be corrected. The most recent concerns a newly formed baseball team playing in Marston Green called the 'Maple Leafs' who have quoted in various documents and on their web site that the Canadians from the wartime Canadian Military Hospital were responsible for the setting out of the original baseball pitch on the 3Ms ground. This is certainly not true.

Baseball at Marston Green was played by the 'Durex Abrasives' (the earlier name of the Minnesota, Mining and Manufacturing Company) before the war and played regularly on their sports ground on Sunday afternoons. As they were an American Company there were a number of Americans in their team.

Sid Bisset was the 'pitcher' and 'Breezie' Thompson was the 'catcher' (or whatever else they called him). They were undefeated in pre-war days in a Midland League during their time playing at Bickenhill Road. They were challenged by an Oxford University team in 1940, who were also undefeated and dominated by Americans. The result was a draw 1-1 which was remarkable for a baseball match. I believe that was the last game of baseball played then as the Americans (who were not in the war at that time) all went home. It was 'Durex Abrasives' who laid the original diamond.

A statement was made in another reference that 'Stirling Bombers' were assembled at the 'Metropolitan Cammell' Factory in Bickenhill Lane (now the Elmdon Trading Estate). The Stirling Bombers were in fact assembled at a shadow factory built specifically for 'Shorts' in 1939 and at the time this information was top secret and not generally known in the village. I don't think the 'Stirling Bombers' were first seen until 1942.

I joined the Royal Navy early in 1945 and when I returned to civvy street in January 1948, only then were 'Metropolitan Cammell' arriving at 'Elmdon' when they had commenced transferring their Bus Manufacturing Division to the then redundant 'Stirling' site. During the war 'Metropolitan Cammell' made tanks not aircraft.

My earlier book was based upon information that I believed to be correct at that time, and later found to be doubtful. I will attempt to correct as much as possible in updating the contents to show present day Marston Green and as much background to the changes that have occurred over the years as possible for comparison.

I now have copies of the Ordnance Survey Map of 1880 which give factual confirmation of the layout of the roads and premises in the village at that time, whereas in my earlier documentation items were mentioned but evidence was not available.

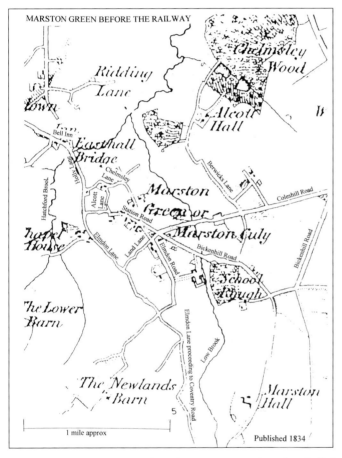

The 'break up' of the 'Digby Estate' in 1919 and 1923/25 resulted in the post war (1914/1918) building in the village, and sadly the demise of so many old farms and cottages which transformed for ever the concept of a small 'Saxon' hamlet.

'Merstone Culi' was built more or less on a sand capped ridge with a stream on both sides. There has always been an old saying that 'to leave Marston Green one must go downhill and cross water'. Until the brooks were deepened and culverted in the early 1950s (thanks to the Airport) Marston Green was often isolated in rainy periods, when extensive flooding closed access to the village at 'Low Brook' where it crossed Bickenhill Road and Coleshill Road, and Hatchford Brook close to the 'Bell Inn'.

These brooks were, in fact, the natural boundaries of the present day village. The northern boundary at 'Eastern Bridge' was and still is the boundary to the City of Birmingham, whilst 'Low Brook' was the southern boundary separating early Merstone Culi from the other pre-conquest neighbouring hamlet of Marston Wavers.

Chapter 3

EARLY DAYS

ACCORDING TO Church Records, Marston Green in Saxon times was owned by Aluric. After him came the Romans and there we find a reference in the Domesday Book to Merstone which means 'Marsh Farm'. There were in fact four local references to Merstone in the Domesday Book with hamlets in the Coleshill and Lea Marston areas being mentioned. But a more positive identification cited 'Merstone being next to Bickenhill and Elmdon'.

Later in 1262, in the reign of Henry III, according to the Assize Rolls, there is a reference to 'Merstone Culi' with land under the ownership of Ralph de Culi, hence Merstone Culi. The manor remained in the hands of the Culi family until 1347 when Sir Fouk of Bermingham is mentioned. Later a Robert Leecroft purchased the whole 'Manor Farm' from Thomas Roche in 1398. Thomas Roche had acquired the land through his wife Elizabeth who was the heiress of Thomas de Bermingham, descendant of Sir Fouk.

The manor remained in the stewardship of the Leecrofts, until Anne, daughter of a William Leecroft married a John L'isle. Their son sold it in 1534 to Reginald Digby of Coleshill. In 1605 in the reign of James VI, a member of the Digby family brought discredit upon the family by being involved in the Gunpowder Plot with Guy Fawkes to blow up Parliament. Lord Monteagle a Catholic peer who had declared his loyalty to King James received an anonymous note urging him to stay away from the opening of Parliament on November 5th because 'God and man would deliver a terrible blow'. The plot was thus thwarted, another Warwickshire man, Robert Catesby and three others were shot and Guy Fawkes and six others were arrested and later hanged.

The Digby family remained squires of the area and during the mid 1660s extended their influence locally by purchasing land and farms around the area, and then renting vast numbers of properties back to the original owners. During the period mid to late 1800s, several of the farms and properties in the Marston Green area came under the ownership of the Digby family and became part of their Coleshill Estate.

In 1862 they purchased the 'Wesleyan Chapel' (the 'old' St.Leonard's) in Station Road which at that time was opposite to 'Ash Tree Cottage' the local hostelry in the village. This was not to the liking of John Wingfield Digby, who was the 'Squire' at the time and so he made land available further along Station Road to build a new local inn, which was named the 'Tavern'. However, later the family were burdened by double death duties, and in the period 1919/1923 it became necessary for them to sell off many of their holdings in land and properties particularly in the Marston Green area.

Marston Green as we know it today, has derived from the amalgamation of and growth of two 'pre conquest' manors of 'Merstone Culi' and 'Marston Wavers'. 'Merstone Culi' was centred around the present junction of Alcott Lane and Station Road, whilst 'Marston Wavers' was situated around the former mansion house of 'Marston Hall'. We still retain a long standing continuity with those days by way of a point in the village which was known in those days as 'Culey Place'. This was at the bend in Chelmsley Lane where it meets Wood Lane which was earlier the main thoroughfare from the village to 'Alcott' and 'Chelmsley Woods' and through to 'Coleshill'. There is also reference to 'Culey Corner' on an Ordnance Survey of 1880 which pinpoints it off Bickenhill Lane on an old track which went into the wooded 'Bickenhill Plantations' roughly where 'Birmingham International Railway Station' is situated today.

MEDIEVAL MERSTONE

The inhabitants of medieval Merstone were farming folk and went about on horseback or by wagon. Many of those earlier inhabitants' names are in the Church Records at 'St.Peter's Church' at Bickenhill which date back to Tudor times. The only place of worship in the village of Merstone Culi was at 'St.Leonard's Chapel' the location being adjoining 'Chapel House Farm' which was off Elmdon Lane just beyond the present Railway Station. This is shown on the Ordnance Survey map of 1880 but despite this, other records have indicated that there was also another Chapel at Lyndon of the same name.

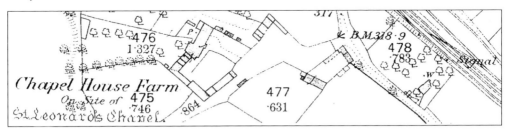

Many years ago I was told on many occasions, from different sources, and older residents did believe it, that in those days there was a 'fraternal' link between 'Olton Priory' and 'Maxstoke Priory'. Monks used to pass through Marston Green, stop at that 'St.Leonard's Chapel', pass through the village via the 'Donkey Path' at the top of the Recreation Ground (suggesting this was the transport method of the monks) hence the name. Continue along the old Berwicks Lane to 'Alcott Woods' past 'Alcott Hall', through 'Chelmsley Woods' cross the main Chester Road (not tarmacked in those days) onto a rough track, now Green Lane and thence to Coleshill, and on to

'Maxstoke Priory'. It is known that the roads mentioned in those days were merely tracks from farms to Manor Houses or Monasteries and were the only highways.

In 1760 during the times of George III, travellers coming to Merstone Culi would have alighted from a horse drawn coach on the old 'turnpike' Road from Coventry. They would have strolled down present day Bickenhill Lane, (under the old name of Wavers Road) and probably rested at a place of refreshment at the old 'malt house' where you can still find Malt house Row. The names of the farmers in those days were Peter Cleave, Henry Faustian, John Holmes, John Smallbrook and Thomas Cannon.

Looking at the Ordnance Survey Map of 1880 below, which clearly shows the farms and cottages that were in the village of 'Merstone Culi' all those years ago, it is apparent that the 'track' layout (which is what they were in those days) then has been determined by the position of the numerous farms. The only means of travel would have been by 'horse drawn' wagons or 'coaches'. We know that mail came to Coleshill by 'Stage Coach' from London which also carried passengers.

It is remarkable therefore, that 130 years later we are still travelling on the same roads that were probably established 200 to 300 years ago when the farms were built. It is interesting to see that almost every road was extensively tree lined and apparently most of them were oak and from observation they also were very old.

Down Coleshill Road in the left hand hedge row you can still see the old tree trunks, and at the far end of Bickenhill Road where new housing has not been so intense there are many that have survived.

When housing developments in 1910 and 1925-6 came along, following the break up of the 'Digby Estate' then sadly many hundreds of established trees must have disappeared.

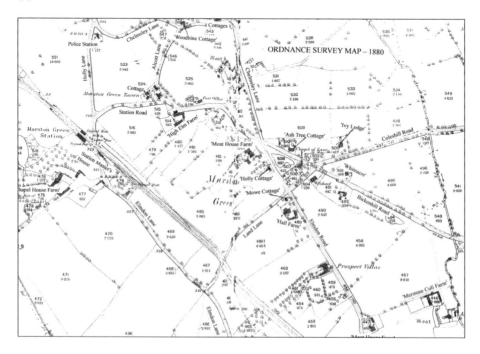

Chapter 4

THE OLD FARMS

IN EARLIER days the farms in the area provided employment for many of the villagers of old 'Merstone Culi'. From the 1841 Census there were 43 properties listed and a resident total of 302 people. Of the total, 187 either lived on a farm or were involved in agricultural activities. There were 148 under the age of 15 (which included 3 sets of triplets) but not many of them would have received any schooling in those days as the 'Education Act' did not become law until 1870, which made education of children 'compulsory but not free'.

Other employment activities recorded, 5 families where the 'wage earner' was listed as 'railway worker', a family of 5 listed as 'policeman', a family of 4 quoted as 'shoe maker', a family of 4 listed as 'clerk' and another family of 4 listed as 'innkeeper'. There was a 'pauper' quoted but sadly there were only 7 villagers listed over the age of 65 which indicated that long life expectancy was not extended to many in those days.

1919 'Marston Hall Farm'.

The largest farm in the village was 'Marston Hall Farm' an excellent building dating back to Tudor times and which covered 224 acres which later was bisected by the London to Birmingham railway line.

The farmer at the time of the break up of the 'Digby Estate' in 1923 was Mr. H.J.Cattell and his annual rental fee was £293.4 shillings and 10 pence (£293.25p). The land of 'Marston Hall Farm' was farmed up to the 1960s at which time the outbuildings were demolished to make way for new terminal buildings at 'Birmingham International Airport'.

The farm and a Tudor Mansion House called 'Marston Hall' were situated at the end of a long elm tree lined drive off Bickenhill Lane which started more or less where the overhead rail track between the Birmingham International Station runs to Birmingham International Airport and crosses Bickenhill Lane.

The house stood facing the long drive off Bickenhill Lane. There were two old cottages at the head of the drive, one of which was called 'Lavender Cottage'. 'Marston Hall' was extensively restored after the 1914/1918 War and during this restoration an old 'Minstrel's Gallery' was discovered and there were many other features of interest found at the same time. Considering the apparent size of the 'Hall' there were only 4 bedrooms,

1919 'Marston Hall' the Tudor Mansion House.

one bathroom, a servant's bedroom and two attics. It does however make mention of two good cellars. Both of the buildings were demolished in the early 1980s due to ongoing expansion and improvements with Airport buildings.

Further along Bickenhill Lane just short of the Coventry Road (A45) stood another Tudor farmhouse called 'Hurdle Hall Farm'. Due to the proximity to what was then known locally as 'Elmdon Airport' this farm was probably the first building to be demolished immediately after the 1939/1945 War.

The second largest farm in the village area was 'Chapel House Farm' and it was said that it took its name from the 'St. Leonard's Chapel' previously mentioned under 'MEDIEVAL MERSTONE'. It amounted to 214 acres from a location off Elmdon Lane some 50 yards past Marston Green Station and all of the farm land extended from the

The once elegant 16th Century 'Marston Hall' the main 'Manor' house of the adjoining 'Marston Wavers' parish area immediately prior to demolition in early 1980s.

In 1935 there were proposals submitted for a new Birmingham Municipal Golf Course on land at 'Chapel House Farm'. In the next two or three years some preliminary work was carried out but had to cease due to the outbreak of the 1939/1945 War.

1965 'Chapel House Farm' immediately prior to demolition to make way for Airport developments particularly in respect of runway extensions. By this time the Marston Green golf course had closed and been replaced by the 'Hatchford Brook' Golf Course built on land off the Coventry Road between Sheldon and Elmdon.

railway across into the parishes of Sheldon, Elmdon, and Bickenhill. It was a large working farm with several 'cow houses', a 'boiling house', an 'engine house' a variety of barns and is quoted in the 'Digby Estate' sales literature of 1923 as having 'picturesque grounds, a boating pool, a spinney and a dell'.

When 'Elmdon Airport' came into service the farming activities were dramatically reduced.

A farm which was situated more or less within the village centre was 'Malt House Farm' which was on Station Road where it merged with Elmdon Road. It was not as large as the previous farms mentioned and only extended to 139 acres. It took its name from a dwelling called 'Malt House' which stood on the same site. There was a gravel forecourt which frontage had a low wall and picket gate which led to the front doors of the farm and the house. There were substantial stables on one side of the forecourt and cow sheds, piggeries and an ancient barn on the other.

The front door of the farm opened on to a typical farmhouse living room with built in 'settle', 'bacon racks', 'ham hooks' from the ceiling and a wide open fireplace with hobs on each side. Down a shallow step, one passed into the parlour which had windows looking out onto the 'rick yard'. The house was built much later than 'Chapel House Farm' and in the 1841 Census it was farmed by Mr. Thomas Cartwright, but in later years was farmed by the 'Hall' family.

The layout details above came from a document written by Mr. Thomas Onley who was born in 1875 at 'Ash Tree Cottage' in Station Road at the corner with Coleshill Road which he indicates was the local 'Tavern' at that time.

In the picture overleaf, the photograph taken in 1920, the building shown on the left is 'Poole Cottage' and is still standing. It is not thought to be as old as 'Malt House

Farm' but when extensions were carried out some 20 years ago the left hand boundary wall of the old farm was utilised for support.

1920 'Malt House Farm'.

The picture above is a print of a painting by a W. Cartwright in 1891 but unfortunately despite extensive research, we have not been able to find any record of the artist. However, in the 1841 Census it is known that a Thomas Cartwright was the farmer associated with 'Malt House Farm' and it is also recorded that when the farm was built it took its name from a dwelling which was already there on the site. Considerable detail is known from information given on the 1923 sale notices of the 'Digby Estate' of individual farms, but none of them describe any dwelling similar to that on the painting. It may well be that the painting is 'Malt House' taking into account a possible relationship between the two 'Cartwrights'.

Nearer to the village centre we still have Malthouse Row which years ago had a row of 6 very basic terraced cottages. These were apparently built primarily to house

1930 The old cottages that stood in Malthouse Row. Originally there were 6 cottages, only one survived demolition in 1960s.

1997 The surviving cottage in Malthouse Row. It did have extensive modifications and improvement including a new roof.

local farm workers due to lack of lodgings accommodation available in the area at the time. There were two rooms downstairs and two bedrooms. When they were built there were no services laid on, there was no sewage disposal and water would have been from a communal pump at an artesian well.

Considering how small the cottages were the numbers living in each property documented in the 1901 Census was quite surprising. They were listed as William

1936 The remains of the old barn which fronted Station Road with 'High Elm Farm' in the background, George Griffin was the gentleman standing on the rubble. An extension was made to the Griffin's Garage which existed for some years with an extensive workshop and repair capability. Later when the Griffins retired 'Jet' took over, the workshop amenity disappeared and today like other garage forecourts sells confectionery, cigarettes and an extensive range of food merchandise.

Whitmore – family of 7, Thomas Savage – family of 8, Arthur Southam and wife, William Ingles – family of 3, Eliza Britt – family of 6 and Joseph Austin – family of 3.

'High Elm Farm' was another old farm dating back to Tudor times. The front door opened out to a box porch, and there were 'spy holes' on each side of the door, similar in design to those found in the old hall at Packington. There was a heavily buttressed wagon shed and a long barn on the Station Road frontage. In the 1901 Census the 'Chataway' family were the farmers and by the standards of other farms in the area it was small and only extended to 73 acres, but later in the mid 1930s the farm was demolished to make way for Elm Farm Avenue and at that time 'High Elm Farm' was farmed by the 'Bracenell' family.

Further through the village in Elmdon Road was 'Hall Farm' which extended to some 117 acres upwards towards the railway and bounded on the village side by Land Lane. This farm was in reality an ancient and modern mix, as at some time the front section had been added to an older building. The farmer was Edward Hall with his 3 sons. The farm was demolished in the 1930s and the land towards the railway was later to become Hall Drive.

When the farm was demolished and for some years after until early 1960s a barn and several outbuildings remained. The barn housed 2 horse driven milk floats owned by the local milkman Harry Biddle who used to deliver fresh milk straight from the farm to the houses which he ladled directly from old fashioned milk churns. At that time there were a variety of small tradesmen who operated from the outbuildings, painters, carpenters, a french polisher amongst them.

Further down Elmdon Road was 'Prospect Villas' which was built in 1870 and it has been stated that these buildings were the "first to be built in Marston Green not having any affinity to agricultural intentions".

Opposite the far end of Malthouse Row stood 'Brierley's Farm' another

1920 'Brierley's Farm' later 'Chelmsley Farm'.

A watercolour painting of the farm opposite Malthouse Row with other old properties visible in Chelmsley Lane beyond the farm.

2009 'Chelmsley Farm' now a private residence. Since the property ceased to be a working farm, the barns and other outbuildings have been renovated and converted into 2 bedroomed terraced apartments.

Tudor style building. Some early records refer to it as 'Greenlys'. When the 'Cottage Homes' were built in 1878 the farm was taken over and improvements made. The 'Wilsons' were the family in residence at the time. Many of the older buildings were demolished and new farm buildings erected. Later John Musson was appointed to the farm and he remained there right up to the hospital (later 'Chelmsley Hospital') was closed.

There were a number of farms on the south side of the village which included 'Gorse Farm' in Coleshill Road, 'Berwicks Farm' in old Berwicks Lane, 'Heath Farm' (also called 'Coleshill Heath Farm'), and 'Birch Croft Farm' in Black Firs Lane. Even further out on the Chester Road (A452) were two large farms, one on the Coleshill side of the road towards Stonebridge farmed by the 'Oakley Saunders' family and the other on the near side of the road farmed by the 'Seymour Smith' family. Both have long since gone but ruined barns of the 'Saunders' farm can still be seen on the way to Coleshill, whilst the 'Seymour Smith' farm disappeared under the joint N.E.C. and 'Birmingham International Railway Station' complex.

The old 'Birch Croft Farm' buildings in Black Firs Lane were demolished in 1994 to make way for N.E.C. Car Parks. It was positioned more or less opposite the 'Little Owl' Public House but immediately adjacent to the wooded area bordering the dual carriage way which turns back to the N.E.C. In earlier days the farm in Black Firs Lane was called 'Rabbit Warren Farm'. In 1938 Thomas Howard Webb is recorded as the resident farmer of 'Birch Croft Farm'. Later Jack Wright and family took over the farm. The 'Wrights' were dairy farmers having over 100 cattle in their herd and they had a thriving milk round. When the farm closed the 'Wright' family moved to 'Heath Farm' in Coleshill Heath Road.

1992 'Birch Croft Farm' shortly before demolition.

2009 'Alcott Hall Farm' which today stands to the right of Moor End Avenue at the junction with Berwicks Lane.

The farm was a working farm which stood on the 'track' between 'Alcott Woods' and 'Chelmsley Woods'. The building is dated as 1750 in the 18th Century and earlier there was a mention of 'Aldcoten' (old cottages) in the 13th Century. A manor called 'Oldescotehalls' was there in the 14th Century and by the 15th Century mention was made of 'Aldectenhall'. In 1692 the records refer to 'Aldcott Hall'.

'Alcott Hall Farm' amounted to some 117 acres and would have extended through the old Chelmsley 'bluebell' woods right through to the Chester Road (A452). In pre-war days the farm was in the ownership of the 'Hall' family and apart from farming they, like other farmers had a milk round and delivered fresh milk in churns carried on a horse drawn cart.

The main route to 'Alcott Hall Farm' was by way of Wood Lane which ran from Chelmsley Lane at a point called 'Culey Place' which was shown on early Ordnance Maps. This was a rough track which ran through 'Alcott Woods', passing through the 'ford' of 'Low Brook' (which still crosses Moor End Avenue) and on to the farm.

1998 'Gorse Farm' in Coleshill Road had been farmed by Harry Musson but since he passed on the farm has been completely transformed and modernised to give 24/7 caring to 14 youngsters with 'autistic' problems. The youngsters each have 'individual' accommodation in converted barns at the rear of the farmhouse, 7 for girls and 7 for boys. The farmhouse is now the reception area, administrative block and contains several offices for the staff. An open day was held when the children were moved in, most of them were, in their way, quite communicative and were happy in helping by handing out sandwiches and 'soft' drinks to the visitors. Everyone in attendance was appreciative, most impressed and in no doubt that a wonderful amenity for these youngsters had been provided.

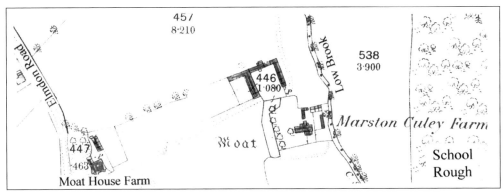

1840 'Marston Culey Farm' and 'Moat Farm' were connected by a rough track which is still visible just before 'Low Brook' bridge in Bickenhill Road. 'Marston Culey Farm' is quoted in the 'Digby Estate' literature as being a small farm of 128 acres.

There was another route, again a rough track which is now signposted as Berwicks Lane. There was just a single cottage on this track 'Gorse Cottage' which was the early home of the 'Musson' family who later on moved to farm from Coleshill Road at the farm known as 'Gorse Farm'.

The farm also had two bungalows on the site and there was a moat fed from Low Brook which was on the village side of the farm. The land which was farmed, extended at the rear of the wooded area off Bickenhill Road known as 'School Rough' and later became part of the 'Bulpitt Estate'. The farmer named in the 1841 Census was Charles Burton.

1967 'Moat House Farm' which stood at the side of the Elmdon Road railway bridge (which was called 'Whitmore's Bridge') in days long since gone. For many years it was farmed by the 'Biddle' family, they were followed by the 'Cattell' family when it was last a working farm.

The farm was demolished about 1947 and for a number of years after some footings of the farm buildings and the moat were still to be seen.

The 'Cattells' had a dairy herd of cattle and supplied milk to local milkmen. The last occupants were the 'Brazier' family at the time of demolishment. Nowadays, Hidcote Grove extends onto the area once taken by 'Moat Farm'.

More recently more new housing has arrived and new roads Somerton Drive – Rotherby Grove – Farndon Avenue and Wolverton Road have extended down behind 'Lyndon Croft' from Elmdon Road.

2009 'Heath Farm' taken from Coleshill Heath Road. The farm was farmed by Jack Wright's family after the 1939/1945 War into the 1980s but farming activities reduced during the 1990s.

*2009 The farmhouse which back in 1923 was called 'Coleshill Heath Farm' on the 'Digby Estate'
literature extended to 119 acres. The farmer at that time was 'Edwin Holliday' and he rented the property
for £146 per annum. The farmhouse was 'spacious' with a Sitting Room having an 'open' fireplace,
Dining Room, Breakfast Room, Kitchen, Dairy and Cellar. Upstairs there were 4 Bedrooms, Dressing
Room and a large Bathroom. Most of the old barns and outbuildings are still there and Jack Wright's
daughter still lives on the premises.*

In 1850 records show that there were 6 working farms and 70 other buildings actually in the 'village' itself. There were also a number of farms of varying size just outside. There were 2 in Mackadown Lane, one on the corner opposite the Railway Bridge named 'Mackadown Farm' and another much further along on the left hand side of Mackadown Lane which was the home of the 'Chamberlain' family. The father

*1930 'Mackadown Farm' was
positioned at the corner of Tile
Cross Road and Mackadown
Lane and in 1923 it was sold by
the Digby Estate and the farmer
at that time was 'William
Harrison' and his rental was
£178.10 shillings. The acreage
was 128 and the farmhouse
comprised Dining and Drawing
Rooms, Kitchen, Larder, Dairy
and Cellar. Upstairs were 4
Bedrooms, Clothes Closets and
3 attics.*

baked bread there and his son 'Archie' delivered fresh bread around the village with his horse drawn cart.

It sounded rather primitive as outbuildings comprised a Coalhouse, a Washing Cistern and Privy but it does add that water supply was from the Birmingham Main. Included in the acreage is 11 acres of meadow land let to Mr. Arthur Betts at a rent of £14.10 shillings.

The farmhouse was demolished when 'Pre-fabs' were erected to remedy a severe housing shortage after the 1939/1945 War.

Across the road from 'Mackadown Farm' was an 'attractive residence' with 'ample farm buildings' amounting to 76 acres called 'Mackadown House'. It was rented by the 'Digby Estate' to Mr. J.T.Redfern and Mrs. Matilda Redfern for £118 per annum. The accommodation of the house included Panelled Drawing Room, Dining Room, Kitchen, Back Kitchen, and Scullery with 5 Bedrooms, Dressing Room, Clothes Closet, Boxroom and 4 Store Rooms.

The farm buildings included 4 stall Stable, 3 bay Barn, 16 tier Cowhouse, 2 Pigsties, another 4 tier Cowhouse, a Bull Pen and 2 Calf Pens, a Blacksmith's Shop and a Rickyard.

In one of the fields was a Barn and Cattle Pen, and in another field an open Cattle Shed, a Mixing House and a Wagon Hovel. Again a note was made of value of timber £122.

At the top of Bell Lane where it met the junction with Tile Cross Road at that time, there was a large farm called 'Tile Cross Farm'.

1920 'Mackadown House' situated at the junction of Tile Cross Road and Mackadown Lane and despite the age of the property is still there today and in good condition.

1930 'Tile Cross Farm' comprised 139 acres of Pasture and Arable land which extended to the rear of the property in the general direction of 'Lea Hall'. This land produced an annual rental of £176 15 shillings. The farmhouse was not extensive in relation to many of the other local farms and included a Kitchen, 2 Sitting Rooms, a dairy, 4 Bedrooms and Box room with the usual 'Out buildings'. Farm buildings included 3 Pigsties, a Barn, a Granary, a 6 stall Cart Stable and a Wagon Hovel. Also in a walled Fold yard were 12 tier and 4 tier Cow Houses.

No details were given on the 'Digby Estate' literature as to who were the tenants at that time but certainly in the 1930s the 'Marsh' family lived there and 'Helen' who I believe was the eldest daughter worked for my father in his Grocery Shop in Holly Lane. She sadly passed on last year at a grand age of 96 years. An interesting adjunct to the farm was a railway coach which stood opposite to the farm more or less where the present row of shops stand. 'Ida' another daughter from the farm used to sell 'home made' full cream Ice Cream from the coach throughout the summer months and used to do a roaring trade.

The farm was demolished shortly after the War to make way for the cutting through of a 'new' road, St.Giles Road to allow for the extension of the 14 Bus Route to Tile Cross which previously terminated at 'Lea Village'. At the same time dozens of Prefabs were erected each side of St.Giles Road.

At the Tile Cross end of the village past the 'White Hart Inn' just a short distance down Gressel Lane was a fine old building which for well over a century was known as 'Sheldon Hall'. In pre war days it was the home of the 'Harrod' family.

A well arranged 'Homestead' with 2 good cottages, 16 acres of Fertile, Arable, sound Pasture and Meadow land extending to 183 acres, the whole of it producing an Annual Income of £288. The 'Harrods' were also considerable land owners in the local area, and quite a significant number of local people were employed at the Hall and on the farm, some living on the premises.

The Hall remained in excellent condition more or less until the 1970s when it became vacant. Sadly for the next few years, it became a target for vandalism. Old

1919 Historical Jacobean (1605/1625) residence known as 'Sheldon Hall'.

1919 The fine old staircase at 'Sheldon Hall' which disappeared during the years of vandalism in the 1970s. The staircase has been replaced, and to authenticate the accuracy of the replacement, a photograph of this earlier staircase is mounted alongside.

1919 Oak panelled Banqueting Hall and original stone fireplace with carved oak mantel at 'Sheldon Hall'.

fireplaces, a wonderful old staircase, oak beams from the ceiling and lead flashing from the roof all disappeared during this sad period.

Later, a gentleman named Brayley bought the property with the intention of refurbishing it, and re-opening as a Leisure Centre, but failed to get planning permission. Nothing further ever came of the project, and the vandals returned. When the present owners took over in the early 1990s, it became a Restaurant and Inn trading under the name of 'Whitbreads'.

Quite recently in late 2008, the Restaurant changed to a 'Carvery'.

Leaving the village by way of Tile Cross Road there were two other farms, one positioned on the left hand side between Burleton Road and Shirestone Road. The other was on the right hand on the corner more or less facing the 'White Hart Inn', and was farmed by the 'Davis' family.

Continuing along into Cooks Lane until it reached the Chester Road (A452), on the far side heading south towards 'Stonebridge' stood long established farm buildings known as 'Fifield's Farm'.

The building does not appear on the 'Digby Estate' literature so it was nothing to do with the farm, and it is hardly likely that a private residence would have been at that location.

1890 'Fifield's Farm' showing the Chester Road passing through the farm buildings and continuing south towards 'Warner's Bridge' which crossed the river 'Cole' on its way to Coleshill. The other building adjoining the farm may well have been a road side Inn or boarding house offering accommodation for passing travellers. Almost certainly they would have been travelling by 'Stagecoach' in those days.

Considering this was the main route to London it can clearly be seen that the road surface was not 'tarmac'. The only means of travel was by horse or by 'Stagecoach' as mentioned earlier, and roads were purely rough cart tracks which normally ran from farm to farm, or village to village.

The farm was just 95 acres in size, the tenant was Mr. George Richards and his annual rental was £95.

On the 1841 Census there are 9 villagers who have indicated that their 'trade' was Farmer. The main farms in the village have been identified, with details as to who they were and where they operated from. These 'other' farmers would have operated from 'pasture' and 'arable' land scattered around the village but probably had no dwellings on the areas.

However, on the 1880 'Ordnance Survey Map' there is one property which can be identified and its location. It is listed as 'House and Stable' and the farmer named as 'Lucy Burton' and the location on the Ordnance Map as 'Bickenhill Road. The property is still there, now known as the 'Marston Green Club Limited' with the address No.8 Bickenhill Road.

How long the building remained as a farm I do not know, but in 1933 my grandfather Arthur James King bought the property called 'Whiteacre' from George Parker who was there in 1920. My memories recall that the rear of the property had beautiful well laid out gardens, with an orchard, a walkway through a floral area with a trellis support for many colourful roses. There was also an area laid out with a full range of vegetables being grown. This area now of course is the 'car park' for the club's members. I think my Uncle sold the property in 1945.

2009 'Marston Green Club Limited'.

By direction of Major F. J. B. Wingfield Digby. D.S.O.

On the Eastern Boundary
of the City of Birmingham

Situate at Sheldon, Yardley, Marston Green, Elmdon, Coleshill Heath, Shard End, Kitts Green, Tile Cross, Castle Bromwich, and Water Orton.

Particulars, Photographs and Plan of the
OUTLYING PORTIONS OF

The Coleshill Estate,

Extending to about 4,580 Acres,

With the Mines and Minerals included, and producing a Rent Roll of about

£6,840 per annum.

The Estate is all situated within eight miles of the centre of the City of Birmingham, and comprises :—

20 EXCELLENT PRINCIPAL FARMS,

Varying in size from **100** Acres to **270** Acres,

With GOOD HOUSES and HOMESTEADS, including the FINE OLD JACOBEAN RESIDENCE,

"SHELDON HALL,"

as follows :

	ACRES.					ACRES.
Lower Barn Farm	147	Shard End Farm	159
The Elms Farm	214	Outmoor Farm	109
Lyndon Green Farm	143	Mackadown Farm	128
Wells Farm, Garrett's Green ...	155	Malthouse Farm	139
Garrett's Green Farm	139	Tile Cross Farm	139
Chapel House Farm	214	Sheldon Hall Farm	183
Marston Culey Farm	128	Kingshurst Hall Farm	269
Elmdon and Newland Farms ...	253	Cocksparrow Farm	143
Marston Hall Farm	224	Burton's Farm	125
Coleshill Heath Farm	119	Attleboro' Farm	136

10 CAPITAL SMALLER FARMS,

Varying from **50** to **100** Acres,

including Wells Green Farm, Mackadown House Farm, Coleshill Heath Farm, Bennett's Well Farm, Hob Farm.

In 1919 large sections of the 'Wingfield Digby' estate were broken up and placed on the 'market' because of enormous 'death duties' which were imposed upon the family. The gravity and size of this sale is clearly seen by the number of farms, good houses, homesteads, small holdings and choice cottage holdings that are listed. Many of them from the 'Parish of Bickenhill' and including most of the largest farms in Marston Green.

In the booklet entitled 'Discovering Bickenhill' edited by Canon Stanley Owen in 1989 which was published 26 years after the book was first produced, a sketch identified old buildings in Marston Green. A field survey carried out in 1962 indicated that of 153 buildings shown in the 1839 Tithe Apportionment, only 55 were extant (still in existence).

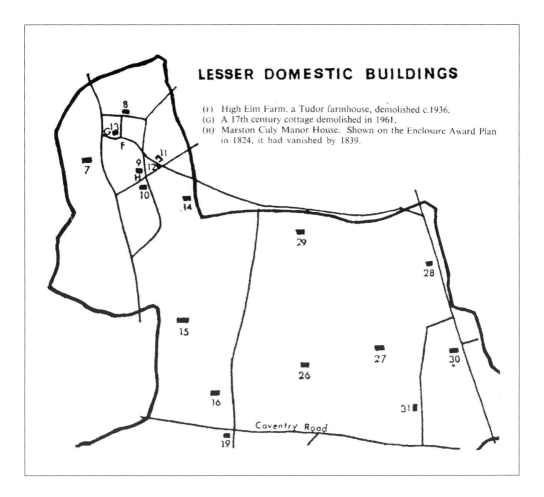

LESSER DOMESTIC BUILDINGS

(F) High Elm Farm, a Tudor farmhouse, demolished c.1936.
(G) A 17th century cottage demolished in 1961.
(H) Marston Culy Manor House. Shown on the Enclosure Award Plan in 1824, it had vanished by 1839.

Coventry Road

Other properties identified:

7 Chapel House Farm, the site of the medieval St.Leonard's Church.

8 Two timber framed cottages, later called Woodbine Cottage.

9 Two Elizabethan cottages made into one, Holly Cottage.

10 Cottage, medieval in origin, cased in brick later called Mowe Cottage.

11 Ash Tree Cottage, the original Tavern.

12 The Chapel, initially a preaching station and Sunday School built by the Birmingham Ebenezer Congregational Church about 1835. In 1862 it was sold to the Digbys who used it as their private chapel. Later they loaned it to Bickenhill Church to enable Marston parishioners to attend services locally. In 1922, they gave it to the Church of England and it remained in use until 1938.

13 The Tavern.

14 Marston Culy Farm or the old Moat Farm, a 17th century house encased in 18th century brick, and formerly surrounded by a moat. Later 2 cottages.

15 Marston Hall, the manor house of Wavers Marston.

16 Hurdle Hall Farm.

19 The Clock Inn.
26 Pendigo Farm.
27 Warren Farm.
28 Common Farm.
29 Birch Croft Farm. 17th century with later additions.

An old property which apparently disappeared prior to 1839, was called 'Marston Culey Manor House'. The sketch map on the previous page does however indicate where this building actually was. Cottage 9 on the map which is 'Holly Cottage' still exists opposite the Memorial Garden, and the 'Manor House' is indicated as between that cottage and towards Land Lane. I suggest therefore that the location would have been roughly where No.7 'Alden' stands today on Elmdon Road.

Apart from the farms that have been identified there are several farms that have long since disappeared. 'Newlands Farm' was up for sale at the first break up of the Digby Estate. At the junction where Elmdon Road meets Elmdon Lane there is an unmade road called Newlands Lane which before the Airport arrived, continued across open land for some distance towards the Coventry Road.

The farm was sold together with 'Elmdon Farm', with the two farms amounting to 253 acres. The farm house comprising 14 rooms with 4 good bedrooms, and the last farmer there was John Suckley. There was also a 2 bedroomed cottage. It disappeared probably in the late 1930s when 'Elmdon Airport' was being laid out.

Another farm was located in Cooks Lane to the left of where the derelict garage stands which was owned by long time residents of Marston Green the Wyatt family. The farm was owned by the Bartlett family, it was a small farm but they had tennis courts laid out at the rear of the property, which I understand were only used for the pleasure of their own family, relatives and close friends.

The garage was owned by the Wyatt family. It remained in business up to the late 1980s but has been vacant ever since. Ernie Wyatt and his father ran the business for some 40 years. Ernie lived at No.89 Station Road, the family home had been at 'Woodgate' in Bickenhill Road next to the Recreation Ground drive.

Two other farms, not strictly in the village were 'Hurdle Hall Farm' and 'Elmdon Farm'. 'Hurdle Hall Farm' (as shown on the sketch map on the previous page) was located on Bickenhill Lane about a quarter of a mile past the overhead rail link from the Airport to the International Railway Station.

'Elmdon Farm' on the Digby sale notice indicated that it had 4 good bedrooms, bathroom, servants bedroom and two attics. The farm was located on the old section of Elmdon Lane behind the old 'Cock Inn' off the Coventry Road, more or less opposite Damson Lane.

Chapter 5

THE OLD COTTAGES

IN ADDITION to the many farms around the village, there was a proliferation of old cottages, most of them brick built with slate roofs, typical of the building style of those days. The majority of them simply comprised two rooms downstairs and two rooms upstairs. They had small windows, were low ceilinged and had low doors under which one needed to duck to avoid head banging. Each had a large fireplace which took up an inordinate amount of space considering the size of the rooms, and there would have been an oven set into a wall used for baking bread.

The cottages had beamed ceilings, and much earlier cottages would have been 'wattled and daubed' rather than brick construction and none of the earlier ones would have been around in the mid 1800s.

Many of the cottages would have had a small plot of land attached, enabling the householder, usually a craftsman or agricultural worker, enough space to keep a cow, goat or a few sheep. In 1875, it is recorded that the village 'carpenter' the village 'odd job man' or 'market gardener' would have held such small holdings.

1930 One of the oldest cottages in the village the 'Whitehead Cottage' which stood to the left of the old 'Tavern'.

In earlier days, the cottage had a 'Pound' or to give it the old name 'Pinfold' which was situated alongside the cottage, and here many of the 'stray' animals found in the village would be 'penned'. Like many villagers, the 'Whiteheads' were self sufficient, they kept chickens, raised turkeys, had bee hives in the garden and also had a 'pet' pig. Teas were served to the 'day trippers' who arrived by train to collect 'bluebells' from 'Alcott' and 'Chelmsley Woods'. The two daughters were Ethel (Morley) and Betty (Harrow), their father was a signalman at the Station, they related that in those days the Station Master used a 'megaphone' to broadcast travel announcements and in quiet periods he would call across to the Cottage to request a record be played on their 'gramophone'. An early example of 'music while you work' giving a clear indication of how quiet the village must have been. The cottage was an early victim to modernisation when it was demolished to make way for the replacement 'Marston Green Tavern' in 1962.

Another old cottage is 'Holly Cottage' still standing in Elmdon Road. In early days there were two separate cottages and the occupants were Fred Loveridge, a night

1950 'Holly Cottage' the home of Joe and Leah Martin.

watchman, and William Carter, the local chimney sweep. The cottages were converted into one just before the last war. It used to have an external 'Brewhouse' until 1958. Post war Joe and Leah Martin lived there. They had two children Anne and David.

According to old records there were 11 cottages in the immediate area of the 'old pit' which nowadays is the 'Memorial Garden'. One that has survived is on the corner of Land Lane and Elmdon Road, generally known then as 'Mowe Cottage' probably because 'John Mowe' and his family lived there for a considerable time'. He was a local Magistrate and his name is perpetuated with 'Mowe Croft' off Bickenhill Road.

In the 1911 Census, John is detailed as a 49 year old 'Signalman' with his wife 2 years younger. I think it unlikely that the 'family line' continued as they had 6 daughters, Annie aged 23, Elsie 22, Ethel 20, Mabel 18, Jessie 16 and Olive just 11.

1920 'Mowe Cottage'. In the photo a 'Nestles' chocolate machine stood by the gate and a notice advertised 'Rogers Seeds'. Buildings in the background were barns from 'Hall Farm'. Teas were available at the cottage with 'McVities' cakes and biscuits.

2009 Present day 'Mowe Cottage'.

John's wife Harriet managed the grocery on the opposite corner of Elmdon Road. After Mrs. Mowe, the shop had a succession of different grocers operating from there. A firm of solicitors by the name of 'Wallace, Robinson and Morgan' came and remained for some 25 years but due to the recession closed in December 2007.

Some years later when John and Harriet retired and moved away the cottage was taken over by the 'Holden' family who had an established glass manufacturing business at 'Adderley Park'.

1920 'Woodbine Cottage' and 'Cosey Cottage' at junction of Alcott Lane and Chelmsley Lane.

The 1901 Census listed 'John Holmes' as a 70 year old farmer with his wife 'Eliza' aged 72, a son 'Thomas' with his wife 'Ellen', both aged 34. They ensured the family line continued with seven children, John aged 10, Eliza 8, Thomas 6, George 4, William 3 and baby Ellen 6 months. The family also had two 'servants' Walter Loats and George Linforth, both aged 16. It is hard to believe that all of that family lived at 'Woodbine Cottage' unless it was a single building in those days. George Linforth was probably the son of Richard the 'Post master' and wife Mary who lived at 'Wayside' in Station Road. Sid Tipper a local builder lived at 'Cosey Cottage'.

In the 1938 Kelly's Trade Directory 'Thomas Holmes' who would have been 61, was listed as being in residence. At the time of the building of the 'Chelmsley Wood' housing estate in the mid 1960s, 'Woodbine Cottage' and 'Cosey Cottage' were demolished to make way for Moor End Avenue' the main route into the Estate. The occupants were 'John Holmes' (the son of Thomas and Ellen) and family, and 'Sid Tipper' and family… I did remember this John Holmes and Sid Tipper!

1900 'Ash Tree Cottage' at the turn of the century. The dormer window which is visible to the left of the signpost belonged to one of the cottages that existed on the small parcel of land known as the 'Pleck' at the junction of Coleshill Road and Bickenhill Road. The horse and cart belonged to A. Cotterill – Family Butcher.

'Ash Tree Cottage' which still stands today at the corner of Station Road and Coleshill Road was for many years the village 'Tavern'. It closed as the village 'hostelry' in 1862 when the local squire 'Wingfield Digby' bought the 'Chapel' opposite, called the 'Chapel of Ease' in those days, and not very happy at having an 'Inn' opposite, made land available further into the village centre to build a new 'Tavern' and in the position where it has remained ever since.

1930 One of the cottages that were situated on the 'Pleck'. They were demolished in the 1950s and never replaced as there was open land in Bickenhill Road adjacent to the 'Pleck'. Later three new 'dormer' style properties were built with small gardens and the 'Pleck' land could have been utilised to give more garden space. The 'Pleck' remains today as an open space with attractive and colourful flowering features in summer months.

1920 An early Post Office (circa 1920 to 1925) in Land Lane. The property still stands opposite the 'Library' and the 'Health Clinic'. It remained as a Post Office until Albert Knibbs married and moved in having previously lived in a cottage round the corner in Elmdon Road. Land Lane as can be seen was no more than a footpath at that time which crossed over the railway bridge.

1950 'Ye Olde Village Wine Lodge' off Land lane and the two old cottages on Elmdon Road. The 'Wine Lodge' is claimed to be over 100 years old and for many years traded under the name of 'Mackie and Gladstone'. At the time of the photo, it had according to the Manager, Mr. C.E.Kirk "recently undergone a major face lift". Alterations included re-roofing, adding oak beams, painted black and white. The 'shoe repairer shop' of Albert John Knibbs was immediately past the two old cottages.

2009 Present day 'Village Wine Lodge' which does not appear to have changed much in the last 50 years. For a few years in the 1970s the premises became an 'Antique Shop' under the management of Janet Henry. In post war days a Miss Bevan lived in No.2 cottage, she taught at a School in Nuneaton during her working life and lived to a grand age of 101 years. She had local connections as she was the aunt of Charles Elliot.

Peter Wilson, a local builder who lived with his family in Elmdon Road purchased the cottages so that his mother could move into No.4. Later Charles and Hilda Elliot who both grew up and spent their childhood years in Marston Green purchased the cottages, despite the fact they live away, they do frequently visit the village on occasions. The most recent licensee is Ruby Marks who greets customers with a 'welcoming smile' and enjoys a chat about old Marston Green.

Charles lived in Bickenhill Road in those early days and Hilda lived across the road at No.7 Elmdon Road with her parents. Her father William Knibbs was the village postman, and Arthur J.Knibbs the 'cobbler' was her uncle.

The shop opened in the early 1930s and Mr. Knibbs was joined by Norman Wilson who later continued on his own until he retired in the late 1950s or early 1960s.

There has always been conjecture as to the ages of individual cottages in the village. 'Holly Cottage' was categorised as being Elizabethan which would mean 400 years old, but other old cottages did appear to have had similar architectural style.

However, not too far away, is No.77 'Fir Tree Cottage'. During a renovation in the 19th Century, a date of 1761 was found carved into the main roofing beams which would relate to the reign of George III.

Thomas Onley, who was born in 1867 in 'Ash Tree Cottage' stated that the two cottages were part of three similar cottages built in the same style. He quotes the third cottage as being between 'Fir Tree Cottage' and two Tudor period cottages opposite Malt House Row. Those cottages were there after the war and lay back from the road exactly where he suggested. The last

2009 'Fir Tree Cottage'.

occupants of the two cottages were 'George Roberts' and 'Tom Essam' and families. The third cottage could well have been 'Malt House' which was part of the 'Malt House Farm' as mentioned earlier.

In the 1881 Census, 'John Penlington' aged 29, lived there with his wife 'Ruth' and their three sons, 'John' aged 5, 'Stanley' 4 and 'Albert' 1. His occupation was stated as 'Solicitor's Clerk'.

In the 1901 Census, 'Frederick Benbow' aged 48, and his wife 'Sarah', lived there with their three daughters 'Frances' (Freda) aged 16, 'Constance' 11, and 'Phyllis' (Dora) 5. Mr. Benbow was a 'schoolteacher' at the 'Cottage Homes'. Sarah died in 1902 and Freda promised her mother that she would look after Dora. Mr. Benbow married again to a woman named 'Clara'. 'Frederick Benbow' died in 1922 and his second wife continued to occupy 'Fir Tree Cottage' as a sitting tenant. She bought the property for £525 in 1924. New houses in the 'Radleys' cost £350 in 1925 for comparison.

In 1935 'Fir Tree Cottage' again changed ownership when the executor of Clara Benbow sold the premises to Amy Taylor (widow) from Walthamstow. Mrs. Taylor had three daughters Esme, Madeleine and Ishbel. The three girls attended the old Marston Green School and Madeleine (later on, Moulds) was with the catering staff at the 'new' school off Station Road until she retired. She now lives in the development off Elmdon Road called 'Elmdon Court'. Mrs. Taylor lived to a grand old age of 98 and it was remembered as a remarkable achievement on her part that she would be seen trimming her front hedge with hand shears past her 90th birthday. Ishbel, whilst the war was on, joined the Auxiliary Fire Service which operated from the area between Station Road and Elmdon Road (Memorial Garden) formed by volunteers from the village and where they housed their Fire Engine. Amy Taylor died in 1981 and 'Elm Tree Cottage' was bought by the 'Haggett' family, they were there until 1987 when the present owners John and Joan Stevens took over.

'Pool Cottage' No.1 Elmdon Road has survived and is situated opposite the village end of the Memorial Garden. It is not thought to be as old as other cottages around the village but can be seen on the photograph of 'Malt House Farm'.

Extensions to the property a few years ago utilised the boundary wall of the old farm to support part of the extension.

At the other side of the old 'gravel pit' were a row of semi-detached properties in Chelmsley Lane built about 1920, which housed the staff from the 'Cottage Homes'.

2009 'Pool Cottage' No.1 Elmdon Road.

37

Further along in Station Road towards 'Ash Tree Cottage' were two other old cottages again both owned by the 'Cottage Homes'.

The Cottages belonged to the 'Cottage Homes', the nearest occupied by Jack and Mabel William's family. They had three sons, Anthony, Raymond and Michael. Jack was an outstanding opening batsman

1922 The 'Williams' and 'Wheeler' Cottages in Station Road.

for the 'Cottage Homes' cricket team, there was plenty of sport played there and they also had a very good football team. It was said in those years, that if you were good at sports, you could always get a job there, (whether that could have been proven, who knows?).

The other cottage behind belonged to the 'Wheeler' family, they had an autistic son named Roy who was well liked in the village. He would always talk to everyone and he loved comics and children in the village made sure that he had plenty to read.

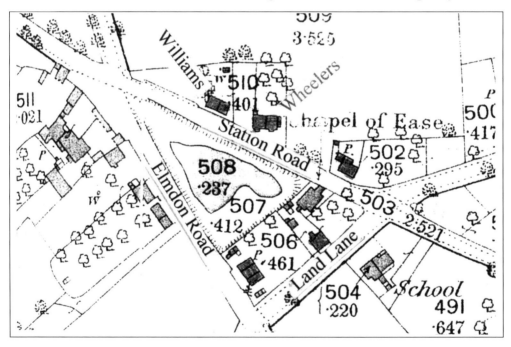

The other cottages shown on the 1880 Ordnance Survey Map are 'Ash Tree Cottage' nearer to the corner with Coleshill Road. It has the letter 'P' alongside it which indicates that it was a public house, which was not so, as the pub closed in 1862. The three terraced cottages shown are in Elmdon Road and the other cottage opposite the school is No.1 Land Lane, all of these cottages have survived. Other

2009 The 'Memorial Garden' with the Hospital replacement modern houses beyond. A bungalow has taken the place of the William's cottage, and the 6 semi-detached new houses beyond were built for the Staff at 'Chelmsley Hospital'. 'Ash Tree Cottage' can be seen further along at the Station Road/Coleshill Road corner.

'Cottage Homes' properties which were built later in the adjacent area near to those shown on the map were on the right hand side of Chelmsley Lane and can be seen below.

The Bickenhill Parish Council 'Centenary Clock' to commemorate 'A Century of Local Democracy' was erected by public subscription and donations in memory of Parish Council Chairman George Aston (1932-1996).

Pre war 'Cottage Homes' houses in Chelmsley Lane.

These semi-detached houses were built for the staff of the hospital, but most of them have probably since been bought by the occupants. Early tenants were the 'Rollasons' who lived in the end house, their children were William, Norman, Audrey and Eric. Neighbours were the 'Longmores' who had two sons, Geoffrey and Paul who were assistants to Bill Adwick at Marston Green Golf Club in the 1950s. Both of them turned professional later, Geoffrey at a course in Norway and Paul, I believe was an Assistant at Copt Heath Golf Course.

2009 Cottages on opposite side of Chelmsley Lane.

Looking down to 'Chelmsley Farm'. The Cottages are not as old as others in the village but were probably built about 1925, the same time as the shops in Station Road.

Continuing down Chelmsley Lane on the left hand side, just before the corner with Wood Lane there is another old bungalow which for some reason was built some 60 or 70 yards back from the frontages of other properties. The bungalow was the home of the 'Billington' family, they had two children, a son Joseph and a daughter Connie.

Continuing to the junction with Wood Lane, which old maps refer to as 'Culey Place' there were three very old cottages. They are shown on the 1880 Ordnance Survey Map, but old villagers with long memories believe that they were much older.

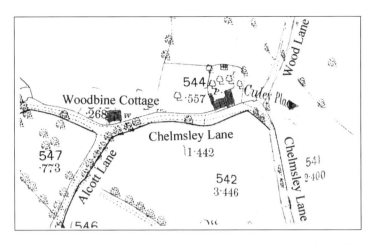

Residents in 1881 were the 'Northwood' family (probably at present day No.48), Charles Northwood, his wife Annie, both aged 25, their children Sarah Marie aged 4 and John William aged 1. The occupation quoted for Charles Northwood was 'civil engineer'. Next door in a terraced cottage lived the widowed mother Jane Northwood aged 60, and her two daughters, Elizabeth aged 22, and Eva Marion aged 14.

Next door lived the 'Chadwick' family, John Chadwick and his wife Emily, both aged 28, their daughter Alica Emily aged 6, a son Ernest Albert aged 5 and a younger daughter Ada Elizabeth aged 3. John Chadwick was listed as an 'engineer in wood' (whatever that was). Ernest Albert Chadwick, born 1876, the son, became an artist of considerable renown in those days. The family later moved to Hampton in Arden.

In the last terraced cottage was Enoch Harvey aged 47 and his family, daughter Catherine aged 16, sons Enoch Richard 14 and George 10, daughters Anne Marie 8 and Florence Mary 6 and another son Thomas aged 1.

Later in 1901 it was all change. The families then were the 'Wheeler', 'Harrison' and 'Dumbleton'. More up to date, Jack Donoghue, a signal box operator lived in one of the cottages from the '30s into the '60s and it is about that time that the cottages were demolished. At that time in the 1930/1940s Leonard and Doris Richards lived at No.48 with their sons John and Peter.

The most recent occupants were Bob Woolley and family and they moved on in early 2009. Bob Woolley believed that the property was as old as the terraced cottages because "between his house and the nearest cottage there was a door connecting the two properties" implying that the two families may have been related, which was

indeed confirmed by the 1881 Census, the family being the 'Northwoods'.

At a point on the corner where Chelmsley Lane meets Holly Lane there is an old cottage which was called 'Keeper's Cottage'.

2009 No.48 Chelmsley Lane, former home of Leonard and Doris Richards.

This cottage was shown on the Ordnance Survey Map of 1880 referred to as a Police Station. Older residents remember this and recall that an early policeman was named 'Chapman'. Whilst this is probably correct, in the 1881 Census a Policeman by the name of John Griffiths was named, aged 45 with his wife Mary, and three children, Hetty aged 7, Elmer 6 and George 2, so it is logical that they could have lived there.

2008, 'Keeper's Cottage' later called the 'Homestead'.

However, I do wonder whether being a Policeman was a 'part time job' in those days. The name of the cottage could have meant that the occupant was perhaps, only a 'gamekeeper'. Marston Green was a small village, generally you would know your neighbours, there would not be a lot of crime and 'strangers' would soon be spotted.

The 1841 Census indicated that the village was comprised almost entirely by farmers, their families and farm workers. On the 1880 Ordnance Survey Map the only building listed in Holly Lane right down to 'Ye Olde Belle Inn' (which was built in 1668, the reign of Charles II), was 'Keeper's Cottage'.

On the 1901 Census there was no mention of a Policeman listed.

I don't believe that general building occurred in Holly Lane right down to the 'Bell Inn' until perhaps 1925, which is when other properties were being built around the village. The photograph opposite was dated as 1925.

Looking at the state of the roadway, it was obviously in the early stages of development. General tarmacing and pavements did not arrive in the village until the early 1930s.

The little track running away at the bottom left of the photograph led to what was recorded as 'Allotment Gardens' on the 1880 Ordnance Survey Map.

1925 Holly Lane looking towards 'Ye Olde Belle Inn'.

In the early 1930s Bob and Peter Moseley whose family had established themselves as Nurserymen took over that substantial area for growing vegetables and other garden produce there. Later on of course, the Moseley family who had contributed so much to the village community over many years with many varied activities that they had been involved in, were remembered when this particular area became a housing development and was named Moseley Drive in appreciation of their hard work in years gone by.

2009 Much changed Holly Lane looking towards the 'Bell Inn'.

Over a period of time in the 1930s, building continued in the section of Holly Lane more or less down to the 'Eastern Bridge' over the 'Hatchford Brook', this being the point of meeting the City of Birmingham boundary. Further buildings followed the style of the bungalows shown but there were a few 3 bedroomed houses later on.

At the other end of the village towards the far end of Bickenhill Road there are two old cottages which appear on the 1880 Ordnance Survey Map but they are certainly much older than that.

On the 1911 Census a Mrs. Mary Leedham aged 56, was living at 'The Heath' with her grandson Joseph Knight aged 13, granddaughter Gertrude 7 and a servant Sophie Deebach aged 28. On an early Marston Green football team in 1919/20 a Joe Knight appears, (could be the right age). The footballer Joe Knight had an Electrical Contracting Shop at the premises now occupied by William Hill the 'bookies'.

2009 'The Heath' in Bickenhill Road one of the two very old cottages.

In pre war days the cottage was occupied by the 'Crees' family, who had two children, John and Adele, they would have been 12 and 10 in 1938. After the war they emigrated to New Zealand but apparently they have returned to the U.K. in recent years due to problems associated with toxic fumes from a volcano near to their home which affected them.

Next door a similar cottage of the same age named 'Heath Cottage' stands. I understand that the Bulpitt family lived there temporarily whilst their house 'East Woodhay' was being built about 1909.

2009 'Heath Cottage' in Bickenhill Road.

In the 1930s/40s a family called Heath Woodward lived at 'Heath Cottage'. They had a son named Sidney who as a young lad worked for my father as an 'errand boy'. He delivered groceries on a bicycle with a 'carrier' attached to the handlebars, and which was positioned above the front wheel.

Beyond the two cottages for many years there used to be stables and it is stated that the Bulpitts converted them into living accommodation which are now called 'The Old Stables'.

2009 'The Old Stables' off Bickenhill Road.

Chapter 6

THE RAILWAY

A SIGNIFICANT event occurred in 1838 which forever changed the 'idyllic' image of rural Marston Green when a railway line from Rugby to Birmingham was laid and passed through the village. The 'London to Birmingham Railway' started as a project in 1824 and there was considerable opposition from stage coach, canal transport operators and in particular 'landed interests'. In 1833, Parliamentary sanction was obtained to build Britain's first major line and Robert Stevenson was appointed as Chief Engineer.

The line cut across a series of ridges and valleys for 113 miles, the cost was £5½ million pounds and took 20,000 navvies nearly 5 years to build, their only tools being picks, shovels and gunpowder.

On April 9th 1838 a line was opened from Denbigh Hall and from Rugby to Birmingham. The line ran through Marston Green on September 7th 1838. A journey from London took about 12 hours by Stage Coach, a Canal Barge took 3 days, a Goods Wagon took 60 hours and the journey by passenger train took 5½ hours. Fares ranged from 1 penny to 3 pence (old money) per ton for freight, a third of the road fare, and 2nd class passengers travelled at 2 pence per mile.

In the early days the track was laid on stone sleepers and at the time it became known that an 'expensive mistake' occurred that for many years remained 'plainly visible'. Apparently, original calculations implied that sufficient material could be taken from the Hampton in Arden cutting to cater for the embankment that was required for the Birmingham side of Marston Green Station. In reality this was a serious miscalculation, and huge quantities of sand had to be taken at considerable expense from fields adjoining the railway.

Excavations were made at various points, and a particularly large excavation was made at the rear of a house in Elmdon Lane called 'Canterbury House'. It is recorded that a 'tragedy occurred' as a direct result of this excavation when a workman lost his way at night, fell into the excavation, which was flooded, and drowned. The large hole referred to was eventually filled in during the 1960s, and at the present day we have Canterbury Drive.

Another fatality, unfortunately as a result of the railway and its bridges being there, referred to the death of 'Thomas Ashby'. He lived in an old cottage in Elmdon

Road and sadly he was struck by lightning on the Elmdon Road bridge. On the parapet of the original bridge, which remained virtually to the introduction of 'electrification', a stone tablet gave the tragic announcement that 'Near this spot, Thomas Ashby was killed by lightning on June 12th 1858'.

Whilst the railway was being laid in our immediate locality, additional accommodation was needed to house the workers. A row of temporary cottages were built in Chelmsley Lane for this purpose and they were called 'The Barracks'. There is a painting in the 'Library' showing these dwellings and the print shown is a copy of the painting. The building on the left hand side is 'Woodbine Cottage' the homes of 2 families called 'Austin' and 'Finden' at that time.

Marston Green Station, more or less until the introduction of a 'bus/rail' connection had a two line goods sidings where Coal Merchants operated their businesses from. George Mellish, and later his son Harry carried on the coal business for many years, and it is of interest that George Mellish was listed in the 'Kelly's Trade Directory' as a Coal Merchant as long ago as 1900. Other Coal Merchants used the sidings and immediately after the war 'Wilson, Carter and Pearson' were there.

The original Booking Office was situated in the sidings. The railway ran lorries from the sidings which used to deliver many items of merchandise delivered by rail on a regular basis. The driver of one of the lorries was a man named 'Smethurst', he was a big man, and my memory of him was his ability to 'single handedly' lift and carry two hundred weight (224 lbs) sacks of sugar, tea and other commodities to my father's Shop in Holly Lane.

On the page opposite is a copy taken from part of the original drawings for the old Station. It is interesting to note that the railway was L.N.W.R. and

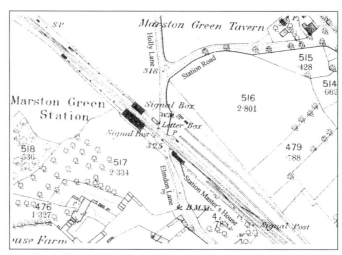

the date of the authorising signatures was October 1880 some 42 years after the first train. The 1880 Ordnance Map shows the Station complete with Waiting Rooms, Signal Box and Male Toilets at the end of the platforms.

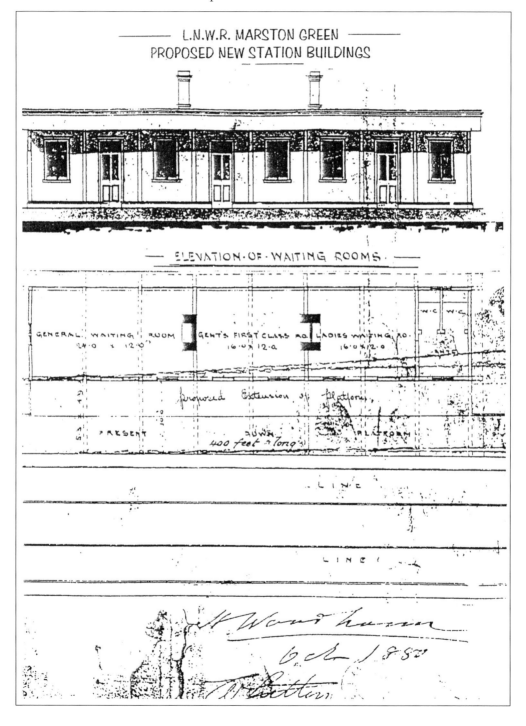

The Waiting Rooms were of timber construction, they were individually heated with open coal fires, and generally trains ran on time. There was a separate Waiting Room for 'Lady Travellers' and they were treated with due respect and had their own flush toilets. The Gent's Toilets were at the end of the platforms and were 'exposed to the elements'.

1920 Marston Green Station.

Long forgotten steam at Marston Green. The level crossing gates and the 'footbridge' were perfect vantage points for children and indeed for adults, who collected 'train numbers', a popular hobby in pre-war days.

Looking down the platforms towards the old level crossing gates. At the rear of the Waiting Rooms on the Coventry side the wooden offices seen belonged to Coal Merchants who operated from there. The small hut just beyond the crossing gates is believed to be the original 'booking office'. Station Staff obviously took a pride in their Station in those days as there were always tubs and troughs on the platforms stocked with colourful flowers and bushes.

1945 The Station before the change from 'steam' to 'electrification'. It was still possible to cross the line to reach the opposite platform without having to use the old footbridge, or to cross from Holly Lane to Elmdon Lane with 'perambulators'.

1950 The 'old' Waiting Rooms immediately prior to 'electrification'. The 'canopy overhanging roof' was removed to make way for the overhead cable gantries. Tickets were available for trains in either direction as both platforms had 'manned' Booking Offices.

1948 The 'sidings' at Marston Green Station with a line of wagons awaiting unloading. The variety of huts belonged to the coal merchants of the period. The houses in the background are Elm Farm Avenue.

1960 Looking in the Coventry direction with crossing gates open. The 'old' bridge was ideal for those collecting train numbers – a very popular hobby in those days.

1960 At the time of 'electrification' looking from Elmdon Lane with Holly Lane beyond the crossing gates. The cable gantries straddled the line which resulted in the removal of the waiting room 'canopies'.

1925 The old Signal Box which was manually operated. The gentleman sitting on the window cill is Harry Mellish, the local coal merchant. Pre-war signal box operators were Sydney Whitehead, Jack Donoghue, Jack Harbridge, Tom Hubbocks and any local youngster who made friends with the operator on duty.

1950 The crossing gates 'open' shortly after electrification. The new footbridge had panelled sides for safety reasons.

Whilst some of the early Station Masters at Marston Green Station were known by name, their respective dates of occupancy had been based upon comments made by older village residents. Whether their memories were accurate or 'hazy' as time has elapsed cannot be determined now.

I had lengthy conversations with 'Rene Watkins' when I compiled my first book 'Domesday to Millennium' on old Marston Green. She was one of the three daughters of Station Master Palmer. She believed that earlier Station Masters before her father were named 'Oates' and 'Wright'.

She was correct with Mr. Wright because he did appear in the 1881 Census. His name was Joseph Wright aged 46, and his wife was Emma aged 44. They had three children, Anne aged 11 at that time, Catherine aged 9 and Thomas aged 4. Mr. Wright was born at Appleby Magna in Leicestershire. His wife came from Staffordshire and their three children were all born in the Parish of Bickenhill implying that they were probably born whilst their father was at that time, Station Master at Marston Green.

There is no Station Master listed in the 1901 Census but there was a Joseph Wright aged 66 with a wife Emma aged 65. This Joseph Wright was listed as 'Coal Agent' and it is plain he was the same man. It is possible that he may well have been doing two jobs, but more likely that he had to retire at the age of 65.

Rene Watkins was aware that her father was Station Master from 1908 until 1930, Mr. Wright therefore could have been Station Master from an unknown date, at least before 1870, to 1900. He could have been followed by Mr. Oates from 1900 to 1908 who was there in that period but too late for inclusion in 1901 Census.

The next Station Master was Mr. William George Weaver who took over in 1932. His wife was Alice Amelia and they had 5 children, 2 boys Richard and Alec, 3 daughters Doreen, Margery and Dorothy, Mr. Weaver was Station Master from 1932 until 1947.

Elsie Palmer, recently died in May 2008 at the wonderful age of 95 and her elder sister died a few years ago aged 97. Must be beneficial to one's health being a daughter of a Station Master.

Station Master Weaver's daughter Dorothy still lives in the village and is married to Ron Wilson, a long time villager who was born at the old 'Tavern Inn' where his grandfather was the Licensee. Dorothy has a long way to go yet to match the Palmer daughters. I hope that she makes it!

1925 The Station Master's House. The lady sitting outside is Mrs. Florence Palmer, his wife and the three daughters are Elsie, Rene and Winifred.

1925 The Station Master's wife Mrs. Florence Palmer returning to the doorway of their home with her shopping, obviously 'camera shy'.

1935 The approach to Marston Green Station with the Crossing Gates, the Signal Box and the old 'up and straight over' footbridge clearly evident. The crossing gates closed in the 1960s. The newsagent at the 'Kiosk' was Mr. Smith, a sign indicated that he sold 'Kunzle' cakes. The signboard by the fence indicated that a 'Lending Library' was available and cycles could be stored. The service was well used and there were ample cycle racks at the rear of the premises.

1994 'New' Marston Green Station from the same viewpoint. Another newsagent, street lamps were introduced in 1938 and a bus/rail interchange had been introduced at the Station.

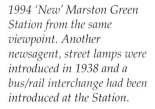

The newspaper boards stated: 'Britain to make Arms Statement' – 'Roosevelt's Dramatic Appeal' and 'A Big Cut in Petrol Prices' (presumably they encouraged motorists in those days). Petrol was one shilling and 1½ pence a gallon (6p).

The chaos that came in with the 4.27

JUNE 1963. Marston Green Station was virtually wrecked when wagons from a fast freight train were derailed and flung both sides of the Station. Fortunately, no one was hurt in the accident which happened at 4.27 a.m. on Thursday 27th June, but trains between Hampton in Arden and Birmingham ceased running. The derailed wagons at the rear of the 12.15 a.m. 'Willesden to Curzon Street' train, were dragged along by the train and one wagon removed brickwork from the Signal Box.

Another hurtled over a platform, down an embankment on to the Marston Green Municipal Golf Course. The wooden canopy over one platform was wrecked, one wagon finished on the platform and another wagon crashed into the booking office at the 'City' side of the Station.

The train was laden with meat carcases which were left strewn along the track and platforms. The level crossing was blocked to road traffic and a diversion was set up through the village to reach Elmdon Lane.

Local residents had a perfect 'bird's eye view' of the salvage work after the train derailment at Marston Green Station from the footbridge across the lines. The wrecked waiting room for the Birmingham trains was obviously beyond repair.

Workmen were soon busy clearing debris after the train derailment had ripped this gaping hole in the bottom of the signal-box.

1990 The 'new' Station Booking Office on the 'down' line to Coventry, serves tickets for both directions. The bus/rail terminus can be seen behind with cars further beyond the terminus 'turning circle'.

1990 The open fronted 'shelter' for passengers proceeding to Birmingham with the 'bund' of the Airport supposedly screening the village from 'undue' noise level in the background.

1990 Marston Green Station looking towards Coventry with the nearest 'crossing the line bridge' for those passengers to Birmingham from the village.

1990 The view looking towards Birmingham with the 'ramped' bridge offering the only way to be able to cross the line for passengers with 'cycles' or 'perambulators'.

Chapter 7

MARSTON GREEN CHURCHES

W AY BACK in 1347, in the reign of Edward III, church records state that "Sir Fouk of Bermingham granted a special licence to Ranulph Leyecroft and Henry de Aumberlee, who proposed to rent 2 yards of land at twelve shillings a year, for the endowment of a 'Chantry' in the Chapel of St.Leonard of the hamlet lying therein for the maintenance of a priest to celebrate Divine Service here and every day in the Chapel of St.Leonard, for the health and soul of him, the said Ranulph, and of his ancestors and all of the faithful deceased".

This chapel is reputed to have stood adjacent to Chapel House Farm which was located on the Airport side of present Marston Green Station, and can be seen on the 1880 Ordnance Survey Map. The old Chapel still existed in 1549, but owing to the abolishment of Mass in England at that time, the priest was probably sent away.

It was more than 300 years before another Chapel bore the name of St.Leonard's in Marston Green. In 1835, the congregational community founded a Preaching Station and a Sunday School in Marston Green, and two years later, a small wooden Chapel was built in Station Road, opposite 'Ash Tree Cottage'.

It was still in regular use in 1854, but then fell into a state of disrepair, and in 1862 it was sold to the Digby family. The old building was replaced with a brick built one and for many years the Digby family used it as their private Chapel. In 1922 the family loaned it to the diocese of Birmingham, so that Marston Green residents could attend services locally, rather than travelling to Bickenhill Parish Church.

1920 The old St.Leonard's Church which stood at Station Road/Land Lane corner.

The old church was heated by open fireplaces and lit by paraffin lamps. Music at first was provided by a mechanical organ. It played

36 tunes, and now and then, because of a default would startle the congregation by jumping from the solemn chant of a psalm to a livelier melody of a hymn.

The organ was eventually replaced by a 'new' organ donated by Canon Dodd of Yardley in 1885. It bore the date 1808 and was manufactured by William Gray and had been installed at Yardley Church prior to installation at St.Leonard's. Eventually it was restored by Williamson and is now in a church in Trunch in Norfolk. Bill Harrow, sadly no longer with us, remembered as a small boy, operating the bellows for the old organ.

A pulpit stood at the North end of the Church but was removed in about 1920. In 1922 when Colonel F.J.B. Wingfield-Digby gave the Chapel to the Church of England, he also made a gift of three acres of land fronting Elmdon Road, for the 'erection of buildings essential to the religious and social needs of church life in Marston Green' – a Church, a Church Hall and a Vicarage. It was another 14 years before building work actually started.

In 1928, on the death of the Reverend T.C.Barnes the Vicar at Bickenhill, the Church of St.Leonard's was transferred to the Parish of Sheldon.

Towards the end of 1936, the building of the new St.Leonard's was commenced, and in 1937 the 'old' Church handed over to the 'new'. Since that time, the old Church has seen time as a First Aid Post during the war years and it was for some time used as a temporary Library, staffed by volunteer villagers. Later, the younger element in the village used it as the Youth Club headquarters. It was finally demolished in the late 1950s.

1930 Inside old St. Leonard's looking towards the Altar.

The foundation stone for the new St.Leonard's was laid on 17th April 1937 by Colonel Wingfield-Digby, the Church being finally completed at a cost of £4000. The following year the Church was consecrated by the Rt.Reverend E.W.Barnes the Bishop of Birmingham on 28th May 1938, Marston Green then became a Parish in its own right later in 1939.

The Church Bell was earlier situated on the roof of the old St.Leonard's. A new Electric Organ was installed in 1947. Mr. S.C.Coleman was Choirmaster and Organist at that time. The wall at the entrance to the Church is a 'Coronation Memorial' and the wrought iron gates were presented at the same time by Marston Green Girl Guides.

The Vicarage was built in 1952 and cost £3900.

Hector Black and his wife Kathleen for many years sang in the Choir, they came to Marston Green in 1936, and in her recollection of coming to a small village she remembered the "excitement and the hard work leading up to the opening of the new Church".

"When in April 1937 the Foundation Stone was laid and the Sanctuary Cross sanctified, the whole village turned out and 'walked' the foundations, we felt part of

1937 Church congregation at the foundation stone laying ceremony at St.Leonard's Church on 17th April 1937. Amongst those known on the photograph.

Extreme left by the upright: Rev. J.R.McCallum, standing in front of him John Gregory with Margaret Ellis to his left. Front row left of centre: Eric Rollason, Robert Chance and Jean Wilson. Front row centre: George Aston (in beret), Hilda Knibbs with fair hair, Francis Barnett with Arnold Lee behind him with hands on his shoulder. Centre right around scaffolding support: Harry Musson and Norman Rollason to the left, Dennis Webb and Peter Roberts to the right.

The Processional Cross, Altar Cross, Candlesticks and Stalls were designed by, and made under the direction of Mr. A. Gregory of the Birmingham Art School. The original memorial stained glass windows, depicting 'Evangelists and Creatures' were designed by, and for the most part, made by Mr. B.J.Warren.

it and proud to be in at the beginnings of the Church. This was the start of years of hard work. The building of the Vicarage and the installation of a new organ were the priorities, but these were delayed because of the war".

Harry Musson of 'Gorse Farm' was one of the 12 choir boys who sang at the Consecration Service on May 28th 1938. "We couldn't read music and had to practice for months beforehand". Amongst those who sang in the Choir at that time were Muriel Seymour, Ron Wilson, Francis Barnett, Robert Chance, Arnold Lee, Brian Jackson, Maurice Colloby, Sheila Hackett, Geoffrey Barnett, Elvin and Ethel Morrison and Mrs. Pullen.

Harry Musson recalled that at the laying of the Foundation Stone the previous year when the Choir sang for the first time, "all of the children were allowed to lay a brick". For many weeks after the consecration, visiting clergy preached in the church. The Choir had to learn 12 anthems by heart in the next 12 months.

Dorothy Heavan (nee Morrison) sat in the congregation for the Consecration Service whilst her parents Elvin and Ethel Morrison sang in the Choir. When Miss Morrison came to the village at the age of 6, she used to attend church services in the old small Chapel.

One of the curates who served in that period of the Church's history was Canon Thomas Heath and at the time of St.Leonard's Jubilee he was then 90 years of age and living in South Africa.

Mrs Heavan's brother, Arthur Morrison, who served for many years as a Lay Reader in the Parish was the first to be married in the 'new' St.Leonard's on September 2nd 1939.

Since St.Leonard's was consecrated in 1938 there have been just 5 vicars. The first was the Rev. H.Roy Sproule 1939-1958 followed by:

> Rev. Michael H.Zair 1959-1973
> Rev. C.Joe Evans 1974-1981
> Rev. R.P.Heaps 1981-1986
> Rev. Roy V.Allen 1986-
> plus Rev. Mary Whitmore (Assistant Priest 1991-1997)

At the time of Rev. Roy Sproule a young 18 year old Roy Massey came to St.Leonard's as organist and choirmaster. It was his first appointment, and he used to cycle from Shirley and recalled later that he found this "wearisome in the winter months". He was only there from September 1952 until July 1953 and when he received an offer to move to St. Albans, Highgate, Birmingham he "reluctantly" agreed because he could get there by bus. He later became organist at Hereford Cathedral.

On the occasion of the Golden Jubilee in May 1988, Dr.Roy Massey MBE, by then an internationally famed organist who became President of the Royal College of Organists, recalled his early days at Marston Green.

A Mr. Coleman started the Choir, and then a gifted young Choirmaster, Brian Masters raised the standard considerably. "I cannot remember when I heard that the job was vacant but eventually I found myself as Mr. Masters successor. At the age of 18, I was naïve and inexperienced in the ways of choirs, but I think I may have had the edge on my predecessor as an organist".

He remembered that the choir all those years before contained six sopranos, four contraltos, two tenors and two basses, and that it was very much a family affair. Mrs. Sproule was a contralto, her sister Mary Talamo was also a contralto, she married Geoffrey Barnett a bass later, whose brother Francis Barnett was a tenor. Chris Senior and his wife were also both in the choir, as were Mr and Mrs. Goldby. Dr.Massey recalled his awful feeling when he stood in front of this efficient group of singers to take his first choir practice. "I really had no idea of what I was doing, I remember giving a chord on the piano, waving my arms vaguely in their direction and they started to sing. They sang ever so well, and I learnt a lot from working with them".

In 1988 Marston Green Church celebrated 70 years since its original consecration.

St.Leonard's Church Choir in the 1950s.

St.Leonard's Church Choir in the 1960s
Standing: William Potter, Francis Barnett, Stan Goldby, Chris Senior, Mr. S.Coleman (Choirmaster and Organist), Hector Black, Geoffrey Barnett, Mr. Birch and Mr. Clarke.
Seated: Mary Nicholls, Mrs. Senior, Frances Yaxley, (?), Mary Talamo, Winifred Goldby, Brenda (?), Connie Billington and Edie Banner.

1963 The massed Choirs of St.Leonard's Church, Baptist Free Church and St.Peter's Church Tile Cross.

THE BAPTIST FREE CHURCH

The first meeting regarding the formation of a non-conformist church in Marston Green was held in the old Village Hall on 21st September 1923. At this meeting attended by 26 persons, a resolution was passed to commence a work on inter-denominational lines and on such a basis as will appeal to members of all the free churches determined to unite and form a free church for all.

Services began in the same hall on 6th April 1924 but by Saturday September 27th Marston Green Free Church was able to open its own building in Land Lane, although it was not formally constituted as a church until February 7th 1925. However, the land for the building had been purchased in July by Henry Taylor on behalf of trustees appointed by the West Midlands Baptist Association and local folk, from Mr. Wingfield-Digby, who sold the site at a 'generous figure'. And herein lies the root of some confusion over the name of the Church.

In 1928 the Church joined the West Midlands Baptist Association and subsequently the Baptist Union and a new Trust Deed, securing the land and premises to the Association and Baptist Denomination was prepared and signed. These deeds clearly state that the land is to be 'occupied and enjoyed as a place of worship for the service of Almighty God by a Church of Protestant Dissenters called or known as Marston Green Baptist (Free) Church'. However, the Church never adopted that name and all subsequent constitutions state that "The Church shall be known as the Marston Green Free Church". Hence throughout its history, the Church has been known as, and referred to itself as, the Free Church, in keeping with the spirit of the resolution passed on 21st September 1923 – until in 1998 it amalgamated with Tile Cross Baptist Church and became The Baptist Free Church, Marston Green.

Nevertheless, the Church is a member of the local Baptist Association, and the Baptist Union of Great Britain, its deeds determine that its Ministers must be accredited by the Baptist Union and it operates under the rules usually governing a Baptist Church. It is, however, in keeping with many Baptist churches around the country, an open-membership church, meaning that membership is open to all who 'profess repentance towards God and faith in our Lord Jesus Christ, not only those who follow the Baptist understanding of baptism as being by total immersion and for believers only'.

The first Secretary was Mr. R.R.Huddleston and the first Organist Mr. Burden. The first child to receive 'dedication' was Neville Goodhall who lived in Holly Lane. The first wedding brought together Mr. Richard Huddleston and Miss Frances Edenborough. The first 'junior' members of the Church were John Huddleston and Alan Martin.

The services were taken mainly by 'lay men' with Mr. R.R.Huddleston acting as leader or Moderator. A series of student pastors from the Baptist College in Manchester served the church in summer months. The afternoon Sunday School continued until abandoned in October 1959, thereafter the children were taught in Junior Church at the same time as the morning service.

A Boys' Club commenced in 1925 under the leadership of Mr. H.Mellish. Mr. Clifford took over in February 1926, running the club as a 'Boy Scout' movement. Later the church group closed and formed the first of the first Boy Scout troop in the village and the church premises continued to serve as Boy Scout (open troop) headquarters for several years.

The first resident Minister, Rev. G.W.Bevan was welcomed at an inauguration service on Saturday 8th October 1932 and he served the church until September 1939. At about the same time, plans were agreed to erect a permanent Church building at a cost of £4000 but the outbreak of war forced the plans to be shelved.

Rev. Bevan was followed by Rev. M.W.Buckley who was ordained and inducted on October 13th 1940 having served as student pastor throughout that summer. Shortly afterwards, in April 1941, the church building was damaged by an Air Raid with damage sustained to the roof, organ, windows and the electric lighting which had only been installed the year before. Whilst at the church Rev. Buckley married a local girl Miss Marcelle Randall. During his ministry, in October 1944, a timber hut was purchased from the village tennis club and stood until demolished in 1972.

Rev. Buckley remained Minister until moving to Bromsgrove in October 1945.

In 1946 it was decided to purchase a house to serve as a Manse, to accommodate the Minister and family. For this the Church were indebted to the generosity of local builder George Foster. The new Manse was one of a pair of houses in Elmdon Lane which were built by the Fosters and George Foster willingly sold one to the Church at slightly below market value. Present day the Church no longer retains the Manse, the property however does remain and can be identified by the small letter box which exists in the original brick pillar of the gatepost at No.103 in Elmdon Lane.

The same year on June 24th, the Rev. H.L.Stapley was installed as Minister. In 1948 an ex Army hut was purchased with funds loaned from West Midlands Baptist Association to serve as a church hall. Rev. Stapley was followed by Rev. S.D.Cuthbertson who became Minister on July 31st 1949.

In 1954 wrought iron gates were installed with the villagers and the Girl Guides contributing to commemorate the Coronation of Queen Elizabeth II. Two years later, in November 1956 Rev. Cuthbertson moved on to a Baptist Church in Darlington, to be replaced on 21st 1958 September by Rev. R.G.S.Harvey. In 1962 the Church joined with the parish church of St.Leonard's to commence the publication of Criss Cross, the magazine that still serves the community today.

In 1963 it was decided to build a new brick Church which was built by another local builder Mr. J.W.French. The 'new' Church was opened by Mrs. Marjorie Davies, President of West Midlands Baptist Association. The old hut was demolished, but the original church building was retained to serve as a church hall, vestry and kitchen.

The new Church was built for £10,000 of which £5,000 was raised by the enthusiasm and generosity of the congregation who had enthusiastically participated in many fund raising activities.

Bricks were laid by individual members of the congregation at the Foundation Stone Ceremony and two shillings and sixpence (12½p) was charged for this privilege. The Dedication Service took place on Saturday 23rd 1963 and the first Sunday Service took place the next day. In February the following year Rev. R.G.S.Harvey moved on to a church in Northfield. The car park was laid in 1972.

In 1965 Rev. Peter Goodall became Minister, serving until leaving for Rickmansworth Baptist Church in August 1973 and he was superseded by Rev. Richard Taylor in 1974. A Girls' Brigade Company flourished briefly after its inception in 1968, joined by a Boys' Brigade from 1970 until 1974.

Richard Taylor left Marston Green to go to the Six Ways Baptist Church but in 1981 joined the Anglican Church. The same year the church received its first, and so

2009 The Baptist Free Church and new brick built Church Hall (opened 1966).

far only, female minister, Rev. Joyce Turton, followed by Rev. Tony Lewis from 1986 to 1990.

It was in 1990 that the Church first began what became a close relationship with the Tile Cross Baptist Church which eventually led to the merger of the two churches in 1997.

David Barber came to Marston Green as Student Pastor in 1991, and on finishing his training became jointly Minister of both the Marston Green and Tile Cross Churches.

In 2005 Rev. Barber left the now united church, and the ministry was taken up by Rev. Tim Cook from 2007 until the present day.

With short periods of fluctuation up or down, throughout its lifetime, the membership has usually been about 40.

THE CHURCH AT THE 'COTTAGE HOMES'

2009 The Church situated in the old 'Cottage Homes' still exists but in what is now known as 'Pinewood Business Park'. It was built at the end of 1879 and had seating for 500 persons, over the years it became multi functional. It had a removeable floor which covered a swimming pool, dances, film shows and many other functions were held there. I don't know what services were held there all those years ago, but having lived opposite at No.62 Coleshill Road for some 36 years, I was aware that Catholic services were held there after the war, and local villagers used to attend.

Nowadays the church is called the 'Chapel' and it was taken over in about 2006 by a firm called Direct Drains run by Alan Beech and his son, who were previously in Cooks Lane. A second floor has been added and they appear to have amalgamated with 5 other companies calling themselves U.K. Drainage Network.

Chapter 8

MARSTON GREEN SCHOOLS

IN 1870 AN 'Education Act' introduced by Liberal MP William Forster made elementary education available to all children between the ages of 5 and 13 which was 'compulsory' but not free. As a result 'school boards' were initiated in most parishes, to build schools and to supervise local education. Most early schools were built by the Church.

An early school was built at Bickenhill, and it is recorded that Marston Green children attended Bickenhill Church of England School. The children would have needed to walk there, and later a small school was built at Marston Green, originally it was intended for 'infants only' and comprised one classroom with a Teacher's House.

An early 'Headmistress' was Miss Barnett, who later married a Mr. Large. At that time, pupils came primarily from the immediate village, but an old Marston Green resident, William Knibbs (later a village Post Man and father of Hilda who married Charles Elliott) recalled that he attended the village school and walked each day from Tile Cross. In 1897, the 'Jubilee Year' of Queen Victoria, another classroom was added, and that class room arrangement remained until after the 1914/1918 War.

1920 The original school classrooms located at the corner of Bickenhill Road/Land Lane.

In the early 1920s the 'Digby Estate' was broken up and new houses were built in Marston Green along Holly Lane, Elmdon Lane, Station Road and Coleshill Road. This resulted in an overcrowding problem for the existing classrooms. In 1927, four timber constructed classrooms were added and the old classrooms were no longer needed. However, the village population continued to increase and in the mid 1930s, the old classrooms were refurbished and once again came into use. I attended the school then for the first time in 1931 and I did not realise at the time how 'new' they were. It is worth noting that the wooden classrooms were intended as a 'temporary arrangement' but in the event they remained for another 30 years.

1903 An early school photo with Mrs. Tart, Headmistress on the left.

1912 Another school photo with Teacher Miss Cook on the left and Mrs. Tart – Headmistress on the right. Building in background was later a Post Office.

In 1900 there were probably no more than a dozen children attending school. By the early 1920s the numbers had increased close to 100. By 1930 there had only been a slight increase to 118. Hard times! Aftermath of the first world war followed by a General Strike in 1926 with large numbers of workers off work for many months.

Back Row: Mrs. Tart – Headmistress, 2nd left Winnie Palmer, 3rd from right Ciss Dalman, Henry Lanham at end. Centre: Dolly Bloxham on left, 3rd left Margery Barber, 4th left Florrie Bullock and Sid Smith, Ray Crook and Bunt Symonds last three on the right. Front: 2nd left John Rollins, 6th left Tommy Bull, Florrie Simmonds 4th from right, extreme right Helen Marsh.

1935 The Headmaster's House in Land Lane positioned where the present N.H.S. Clinic is situated. Building to the left was the original School Classroom.

1935 The timber classrooms at the 'old' School taken from the playground. The building at the far end was the Headmaster's House.

1936 The 7th Form (Top Class) Back Row: Form Master-Frank Cooper, John Smith and Headmaster Clarrie Bate. Centre: Norman Bowker, Bill Harrow, Joe Billington, Les Colloby and Gordon Davis. Front Row: Ethel Whitehead, Peggy Perkins, Kitty Gallahar and Elsie Jacobs.

Conditions in the wooden classrooms were primitive. Heating of individual classrooms was by way of a coke burning stove which stood in the corner of each classroom. Children received a bottle of milk each day, and these were warmed in winter months around the stove. The toilets were outside, open to the elements, and children had to cross the playground to reach them.

An Education Act of 1944 decreed that schooling should move to a three tier system, with Infant, Junior and Secondary status. This required that children attaining the age of 11 years would move on to the next level of school, be it Secondary or Comprehensive.

SCHOOL SPORTS DAY - 23RD JULY 1938

Programme of Events

ALL HEATS HAVE BEEN RUN OFF.   ONLY FINALS WILL BE RUN ON SPORTS DAY.
AGES AS ON 23rd JULY, 1938.

1.   GIRLS' (5-6) FLAT RACE   1, 2, 3.
2.   BOYS' (5-6) FLAT RACE   1, 2, 3.
3.   GIRLS' (6-7) FLAT RACE   1, 2, 3.
4.   BOYS' (6-7) FLAT RACE   1, 2, 3.
5.   GIRLS' (5-6) EGG AND SPOON RACE   1, 2, 3.
6.   GIRLS' (6-7) EGG AND SPOON RACE   1, 2, 3.
7.   BOYS' (5-6) THREE-LEGGED RACE   1, 1, 2, 2.
8.   BOYS' (6-7) THREE-LEGGED RACE   1, 1, 2, 2.
9.   BOYS' (7-8) FLAT RACE. D. Price, B. Thompson, B. Jones, B. Phipps, M. Smith, P. Troy.
10.   GIRLS' (7-8) FLAT RACE. J. Black, M. Cheshire, B. Whittaker, A. Harrow, J. Hastings, N. Heath.
11.   BOYS' (8-9) FLAT RACE. G. Dale, K. Harrow, J. Hughes, R. Owens, J. Hall, T. Williams.
12.   GIRLS' (8-9) FLAT RACE. M. Kirkpatrick, A. Baldwin, E. Phipps, C. Billington, M. Gallahar, D. Chubb, J. Elsden, B. Phipps.
13.   BOYS' (9-10) FLAT RACE. T. Anderton, I. Davis, D. Rollason, M. Castle, R. Price, J. Thomas.
14.   GIRLS' (9-10) FLAT RACE. A. Brown, N. Clark, B. Lee, D. Mellish, J. Crawford, P. Freeman, B. Sheridan.
15.   BOYS' (10-11) FLAT RACE. D. Belcher, R. Chance, C. Elliott, D. Smith, C. Alford, J. Arnall, B. Biddle, F. Cross.

17.   BOYS' (11-12) FLAT RACE. C. Anderton, C. Hollins, J. Crees, F. Barnett, A. Lee, B. Taylor, G. Humpris, S. Haynes.
18.   GIRLS' (11-12) FLAT RACE. J. Wilson, N. Bowles, J. Smith, E. Gallahar, G. Brown, B. Aldridge, M. Blizzard, M. Everitt.
19.   BOYS' (12-13) FLAT RACE. P. Pemberton, R. Hollins, M. Dreyson, S. Atack, C. Hudson, E. Rollason, K. Wilkes, G. Burgess.
20.   GIRLS' (12-13) FLAT RACE. V. Webb, B. Whitehead, P. Hanson, B. Alford, I. Taylor, J. Wyatt, I. Rollins, M. Popplewell.
21.   BOYS' (OVER 13) FLAT RACE. J. Churchill, M. Musson, K. Dewick, P. Moseley, N. Green, J. Harrow.
22.   GIRLS' (OVER 13) FLAT RACE. H. Lee, M. Taylor, B. Watson, J. Anderton, R. Deeks, J. Chance, O. Beardmore.
23.   LOWER SCHOOL (BOYS') SACK RACE. T. Williams, R. Owens, J. Checkett, B. Skinner, D. Beardmore, P. Harding, R. Hopkins.
24.   JUNIOR GIRLS' SACK RACE. G. Bicknell, J. Crawford, D. Mellish, J. Herriott, J. Marsh, A. Crees, F. Brindley, S. Knight.
25.   SENIOR BOYS' SACK RACE. N. Cowley, I. Davis, D. Smith, J. Gregory, D. Belcher, J. Thomas.
26.   SENIOR GIRLS' SACK RACE. I. Rollins, P. Sheridan, M. Taylor, I. Taylor, P. Smith, H. Lee.
27.   JUNIOR BOYS' SACK RACE. L. Brown, J. Harrow, A. Lee, P. Pemberton, C. Brown, D. Audley, S. Whittaker, J. Devine, B. Keen, S. Heath.
28.   LOWER SCHOOL (BOYS') BALANCE RACE. E. Berry, G. Dale, A. Waite, B. Lee, M. Thatcher, B. Thompson.
29.   JUNIOR BOYS' BALANCE RACE. I. Davis, D. Smith, M. Castle, J. Arnall, K. Mathews, N. Cowley.
30.   LOWER SCHOOL (BOYS') EGG AND SPOON RACE. R. Owens, J. Hall, J. Field, T. Williams, D. Bell, P. Troy.
31.   LOWER SCHOOL (GIRLS') EGG AND SPOON RACE. C. Billington, B. Hollins, D. Chubb, J. Walker, M. Harris, G. Whittaker, M. Cheshire, N. Heath, J. Reading, B. Forster.
32.   JUNIOR GIRLS' EGG AND SPOON RACE. J. Crawford, A. Brown, J. Carter, G. Brown, A. Crees, E. Green, M. Blizzard.
33.   JUNIOR BOYS' EGG AND SPOON RACE. B. Biddle, D. Belcher, J. Pearson, J. Gregory, K. Mathews, R. Chance, V. Keen, J. Davis.

In 1944, two fabricated classrooms were added as a 'war time nursery' for younger children, and after the war had finished these new buildings were converted to create an 'Infants' Department. Further buildings were added in 1952, with the addition of another classroom and a Dining Room.

By 1952, children attending Marston Green School had risen to 300 with ages ranging from 5 years to 11 years.

In the early 1960s, a new School was built off Station Road, the Infants were the first to move and the Juniors followed them in 1964. At that time the 'giant' Chelmsley Wood housing complex had been approved, and it was apparent that the new school would not be large enough to cater for the anticipated extra numbers that would arise

1952 Teaching Staff at Marston Green School Back Row: Dudley Morgan, Lorna Kay, Dorothy Marsh, Barbara Hardman and William Spencer. Front Row: Mary Walker, Frank Cooper, Clarrie Bate – Headmaster, Fannie Harborne and Muriel Thompson.

In the 90 years lifetime of the 'old' School there were only four Head Teachers, Miss Barnett, Mrs. Tart, Mr. Clarrie Bate and Mr. Harold Enstone. Clarrie Bate was Headmaster from 1930 until his retirement in 1958. Harold Enstone followed him as Headmaster and took the School to its new premises in Station Road.

from the Marston Green catchment area. It was therefore decided to build a separate 'Infants' School on the site with an entrance from Elm Farm Avenue.

Since the school moved to the new location in Station Road there have been five Headteachers. Most locals do remember who they were, but I have found it frustrating

2008 The entrance driveway to the Marston Green Junior School off Station Road.

The old school buildings were eventually demolished in 1965.

When the old school closed Harold Enstone was Headmaster and some of the existing staff moved with him to the new schools – Frank Cooper, Dudley Morgan, William Spencer and Mary Walker.

The buildings on the left are a row of new maisonettes which were built around the same time as the new school, replacing a pair of old 'Tudor' cottages which had faced Malt House Row for many years previously. They were demolished in the early 1960s.

trying to ascertain what period of time that each one of them were in charge. Apparently, nobody keeps records for any period of time other than the last seven years. To the best of my knowledge, I believe the five were Harold Enstone from 1959 to 1975, Malcolm Birch 1976 to 1985, June Clark 1986 to 1989, John Dainty 1990 to 1998 and up to date Mrs. Lynn Clarke October 1998 to present day.

2009 Marston Green Junior School off Station Road.

2009 Marston Green Infant's School in Elm Farm Avenue.

The first Headteacher at the time of opening the new school was Jean Thompson and present day is Mrs. M.Parfitt.

Chapter 9

THE POST OFFICE

IN BYGONE days Stage Coaches were the means of transporting mail and parcels around the country, and it is recorded that mail from London came to Coleshill, which was the main sorting office for the Midlands. Mail for Birmingham was addressed as near Coleshill. It was slow and the arrival of the railway gave way to new consideration for distribution.

In 1840, a reformer named Rowland Hill took advantage of the rail network and growing literacy to create a universal cheap postal system in Britain. For just a penny a letter weighing half an ounce could be sent anywhere in the realm. Payment by purchase from a Post Office for an adhesive label bearing the Queen's Head (Victoria) which was then attached to the envelope. Some stamps (penny blacks) are worth a fortune today.

The earliest known position of a Post Office in Marston Green was at a little cottage in Station Road, which was at a location known, (in hindsight) to be on the forecourt of Griffin's Garage, which came later.

The Post Master was listed in the 1881 Census as William Wood aged 61, with his wife Caroline aged 53 and their son Matthew aged 37. In a newspaper article dated March 21st 1953, a Mrs. J.E.Crook aged 84, indicated that she had lived earlier in the cottage of her grandfather for 50 years and that he had been the Post Master.

Taking into account the 50 years she indicated, meant that she would have lived at her grandfather's from 1865 until 1919. If Mrs. Crook's dates are correct then William Wood would have been Post Master from 1865 until 1885 when he retired.

In the 1901 Census, Richard Linforth aged 48 was listed as Post Master, with his wife Mary 45, and their daughters Louisa aged 15, Cecilia 5, and their son Stuart 3.

At this time William Wood was still around aged 81 (and in support of Mrs. Crook's statement) he was living with Mrs Jane E.Crook aged 31 and her husband Albert aged 34, and their son also named Albert aged 5.

Therefore the Linforths must have operated from somewhere else. The 1880 Ordnance Survey Map does clearly indicate that this was in Station Road and information passed on by older residents have stated that this was at a house called 'Wayside'.

OLDEST INHABITANT OF MARSTON GREEN
Mrs. Crook Keeps Abreast of Time

Marston Green's oldest inhabitant is Mrs. J.E. Crook of 55, Holly Lane, who will be 84 in August. Unlike most of the other oldest inhabitants in the various communities of Warwickshire, she does not think that the best days of her life lay in the past. On the contrary, she believes in keeping abreast of the times and welcomes any changes that progress or better living conditions may bring. Mrs. Crook's mother was born in Marston Green and she has lived there practically all of her life. The Crook family have a reputation for longevity. Two months ago she lost her husband Albert Crook, retired horse collar maker at the age of 85. Her grandfather, who was buried at Bickenhill was 86, her mother died at 75, and her mother's sister died at 83.

THE LITTLE COTTAGE

Mrs. Crook lived for 50 years at the little cottage in Station Road of her grandfather William Wood village Post Man and Post Master. Mrs. Crook remembers when the Cottage Homes were built for orphans. It was the erection of the Homes that led to the introduction of gas lighting to the village, and the Crooks were probably the first local family to use gas. "The mains passed our cottage so we asked if we could be connected"' she told our reporter. "Then when the water mains were laid we had a proper piped supply installed".

CANTERBURY HOUSE

Mrs. Crook is one of the few who can remember the appearance of 'Canterbury House' in Elmdon Lane, home of a former headmaster of King Edward Grammar School, Birmingham – "a huge rambling, gloomy place with extensive gardens". Canterbury House was demolished to make way for some of the present houses in Elmdon Lane. All that remains are the gate posts, which give entry to the home of Rev. S. D. Cuthbertson at No. 109.

Wayside and three other buildings were demolished in the 1960s to make way for the new houses (situated opposite the present Junior School Driveway) which were built at the same time and today carries the name 'Wayside'.

The Linforths were listed as Post Master and Post Mistress so maybe because two names were mentioned for the first time on Census the Post Office was becoming busier than hitherto, handled more mail, and the Post Master may well have had to

1940 'Wayside' – was No.40 Station Road.

deliver as well. Richard Linforth would have reached 65 in 1918, so presumably would have retired, and maybe like his predecessor he would have carried on living at 'Wayside'.

The next Post Office was at No.7 Holly Lane which was primarily the 'Chelmsley Drug Store' owned by a Mrs. Louisa Bates who was the Pharmacist. I believe that the property was built in 1910. Assuming that she took over as Post Mistress on the retirement of Richard Linforth she would have commenced in her new capacity in 1918.

She didn't last long though and it was known that an 'officious' Post Office Inspector was not impressed at Mrs. Bates running two businesses, particularly that her Drug Store apparently took first consideration when it came to customers. As a result he relieved her of the Post Office responsibility which was probably before 1920.

The next Post Office was again at a private residence, this time at No.2 'The Cottage' in Land Lane (opposite the present N.H.S. Clinic) and the Post Master was a Mr. Jeffs and he remained there until 1925.

Albert Knibbs who previously lived in one

1922 The early Post Office at the cottage in Land Lane.

of the old cottages round the corner in Elmdon Road, started a shoe repairing business alongside in a small shop (which later became a charity shop called the 'Church Mouse') About that time he decided to get married, he bought No.2 in Land Lane and the Post Office had to close.

The Post Office once again moved, and this time it was just a short distance across the Elmdon Road/Land Lane crossroad to another store on the left hand side of Land

Lane. The store was owned by Mrs. Dora Sharp and according to an old photograph she ran a 'variety' store with quite a selection of different goods on offer.

Looking at the photograph on the left the Postmistress Mrs. Dora Sharp is standing in the doorway and it is obvious that her shop sold other commodities before she took over. It is interesting to note the

1926 The Post Office after it had moved from the 'Cottage' in Land Lane.

'phone box', my first memories of phone boxes in the village were all the old red type which were around for years. This one looks as though it might have been a prototype for the Dr.Who television series which came later!

Once again like previous Post Offices, her tenure as a Postmistress was cut short when Frank Aston arrived in 1929. He bought the premises and opened there with a family butchery business which continued there for another two generations of Astons, Reg his son and George his grandson.

Finally the Post Office made a move to a 'permanent' location at No.1 Alcott Lane. The land was apparently owned by William Bissell the proprietor of the 'Tavern' which was directly opposite. In 1927 Mr. Bissell sold the land to Percy Courts who had the first 'official' Post Office built there.

I was not aware Mr. Bissell originally owned this particular site and sold it to Mr. Courts who became the first Post Master at that location. Fortunately, Mrs. Trish Holden wife of the present Post Master John Holden, was kind enough and patient enough, to wade through some 80 years of property deeds of this property to establish not only Mr. Courts' appointment but also the full list of subsequent Post Masters up to the present day.

Mr. Courts remained there until 1946 when he passed away. At this time the property that was referred to as "dwelling house and shop known as Marston Green

2009 Present day Post Office.

Post Office" passed to his wife Lilian Courts, who for whatever reason, according to the deeds lived in Coventry.

It is known however, that Norman Coltman was the Sub-Post Master after the war so he must have rented the property from Mrs Courts. He would have been there up to 1957 because that year Mrs. Courts sold the premises to Arthur Kibble and his wife Ethel.

In 1960 the Kibbles sold the Post Office to William Adams and his wife Gertrude. In 1961 another sale, this time to Bernard Whitworth Hunter.

He sold in 1966 to Reginald Morris, he was followed in 1969 by Kenneth and Emily Lorton who made alterations to the property.

Finally more up to date, in 1979 the Lortons sold the Post Office to Doug and Patricia Lane with Douglas the Sub-Post Master. In 1989 the Lanes sold out to Brian and Margaret Payne with Brian as the Sub-Post Master.

In 2003 the Paynes moved on and today we have John and Trish Holden with John as Sub-Post Master, they have settled in well and are popular and appreciated by all who need their advice and assistance.

Chapter 10

THE COTTAGE HOMES

FOR OVER a century, the care of children whose circumstances necessitated their maintenance at public expense came under the responsibility of the Authorities charged with that duty. From 1797 to 1852 such children were provided for in an 'Asylum' for the Infant Poor at Summer Lane which had accommodation for 400 children. At the new 'Poor Law Institution' provision was made for a Children's Department to separate children from adults, but the presence of 'undesirable adults' and the fact that the department was within the precincts of a mixed institution rendered other arrangements desirable.

Other options were tried without satisfactory results, so in March 1878, 43 acres of land were purchased at Marston Green and by the end of 1879 several buildings were completed, viz: 14 Cottages (seven for boys and seven for girls) each having accommodation for 30 children and rooms for Foster Parents, a Superintendent and Assistants. There was a school for 420 children, Workshops, Stores, an Infirmary and a Bakery. A Church to seat 550 persons was added in the same year. Two new Cottages for 'Infants only' were erected in 1912, twenty children of two years and upwards were accommodated in each of the Cottages. These were opened by the Lady Mayoress of Birmingham, Mrs George Cadbury.

All the children at the required age attended the school within the 'Homes' which had a staff of fully qualified non resident teachers. On leaving school, boys received instruction in bakery, tailoring, shoe making, carpentry, farming and gardening. The girls were trained for domestic service, sewing and laundry work, those with exceptional aptitude received special training in various subjects for teaching, nursing and one girl progressed to become a Ward Sister at a large London Hospital.

City Water came to the 'Cottage Homes' 1912 as a 'stand by' to the Artesian Well, and a Gas Service from the 'City Corporation' in place of the old fashioned 'oil fired lighting and heating system' was installed the same year.

In the same year a Convalescent Home was made available at 'Ivy Lodge' at the village end of Coleshill Road with accommodation for twelve children, and this new unit, where children went after sickness, proved of great benefit.

In 1924, a new 'swimming pool' and 'Assembly Hall' was built.

1925 The Front Entrance to the 'Cottage Homes'. The 'picket fence' was replaced at a later date with a high 'close boarded' fence which virtually shut off the buildings from the outside world.

By 1928 the accommodation provided at the 'Cottage Homes' comprised:

	Beds	Number of children on 30th June 1928
Boys' accommodation	228	171
Girls' accommodation	219	178
Infants' accommodation	40	36
Convalescent Home	12	11
Probationary Home	18	11
Total accommodation	517	408
Infirmary	32	6

Three of the Boys' Cottages were in the charge of a 'Foster Father' and a 'Foster Mother' and the Girls' Cottages were in the charge of a 'Foster Mother' and an 'Assistant Foster Mother', the whole being under the control of a 'Committee of Guardians' acting through a Superintendent and a Matron.

1996 The Catholic Church at the 'Cottage Homes' capable of seating 550. Over the years it became 'multi-functional', it had a 'removable' wooden floor which covered an indoor swimming pool. Dances, film shows and many other varied functions were held there.

1999 A typical view of the old Cottages at the time of the photograph being taken all of the buildings were empty.

Aerial view of the 'Cottage Homes' with Coleshill Road in the foreground.

Boys and girls were taught swimming and life saving. Football, Cricket, Hockey and Netball teams were frequently arranged. A number of boys were trained to form an efficient Brass Band, which apart from playing at the 'Homes' had regular engagements locally around the district. Others attended Scout's Ambulance Classes and some of the girls were members of the Marston Green Girl Guides and Brownies.

After the 1939/1945 War, numbers declined at the 'Cottage Homes' as the need for such establishments decreased. The name was changed to 'Chelmsley Hospital' and the 'patients' within were either 'mentally incapacitated' or because of 'physical malformaties' needed 24 hour hospitalisation. Cottages became 'Wards' and over the years many of them closed. Finally at the approach of the Millennium the bulldozers moved in and 'Marston Green Cottage Homes' passed into history.

2008 *After the closure, building work took place over a number of years and new buildings were added in a manner to match the 'profile' of the remaining buildings. A variety of companies arrived which adapted the name of 'Pinewood Business Park'. The existing 'Gate Office' remained after refurbishment.*

2007 *'Pinewood Business Park' with the four new buildings 'styled' to compliment the existing 'Wards' of the old hospital. Generally most locals do agree that the end result is satisfactory.*

2009 *The last building of 'Pinewood Business Park' finished some three years later than the other buildings as it was erected on made up ground to counter the slope of the roadway. All buildings are now occupied.*

Chapter 11

THE LOCAL HOSTELRIES

'ASH TREE Cottage' which stood on Station Road at the junction with Coleshill Road was recorded as the first licensed premises in the village. There were a number of other places that locals were known to brew their own beer, but probably only for their own consumption. Tom Onley, who was born in the cottage in 1867, lived to a ripe old age into his 'nineties' and said that the cottage was built at the same time as 'Fir Tree Cottage' which apparently when a renovation was carried out in early the early 1900s, a date of 1761 was found carved into the main roof timbers. If that was the date when erected, it is quite a co-incidence because the licence was removed at the behest of the 'Digby' family in 1862 virtually one hundred years later.

A fresh location was made available and the new 'pub' opened as 'The Tavern' and typified the image of a village pub as from then on many varied village activities took place there. The owners were 'Mitchell and Butlers' and an early publican in 1881 was listed as David Marks and his wife Mary, both aged 45. Entering the front

1910 An early print of the old 'Tavern'. The car park was straight off the roadway, around the tree was a customised bench seat virtually at the side of the road. The buildings on the left were the 'Gents' outside toilets which were not the most hygienic.

In 1901 the licensee was Eliza Palmer aged 64, and her staff were Florence aged 32, her daughter and a servant also named Eliza, surname Fanshaw, (married daughter?)

reception door, one passed into a long passageway which extended right through the building to the rear exit. Casual drinkers used to hover in that area which became rather crowded. On immediate right hand was a serving hatch with the lower door normally closed. Behind the door was the 'Snug' a popular spot for 'favoured' customers who could sit in this privileged position without having to queue for service. Across the passageway from the 'Snug' was the 'Mixed Lounge' the main room, a room about 25 feet square, further down the passage way was a smaller room; the 'Smoke Room'.

At the rear of the 'Tavern' was a brick built store and a large wooden chalet which was a popular venue particularly in the summer months when afternoon teas were served and many social functions were held there. It was positioned to the left of the 'Tavern' towards Holly Lane and looked over the splendid bowling greens and tennis courts. There was a strong bowls club based at the 'Tavern' and matches were played regularly on Wednesday afternoons (early closing day), and Saturday afternoons.

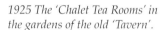

1925 View of the 'match' bowling green with tennis courts in the background.

1925 The 'Chalet Tea Rooms' in the gardens of the old 'Tavern'.

The 'Chalet' was large enough to cater for weddings, private parties and local Sports Clubs used the premises for Annual Dinner Dances. Similarly it was ideal for General Meetings with the advantage of refreshments being available. For a few years in the 60s, one licensee ran a popular Annual Flower and Vegetable Show in the 'Chalet'.

Good exhibits were shown, especially as the Village Flower Show was a day earlier.

A long serving licensee at the 'Tavern' was William Joseph Bissell who was there for many years prior to the 2nd World War and he left to take over the popular 'Three Horse Shoes' on the Coventry Road. This early building was demolished in the late 50s early 60s and replaced with a modern smaller version with the same name behind the earlier one, off Horse Shoes Lane.

1935 The Licensee William Joseph Bissell. The plaques on the wall indicate that N.C.U. (National Cyclists Union) and C.T.C. (Cyclists Touring Club) organisations held their meetings there. The 'carbide' front lamp of the bicycle was well before the days of dynamos and batteries.

1940 The 'Tavern' with the Post Office and the Police Station on the right in Alcott Lane, taken shortly after Station Road was converted from a single carriageway to dual carriageway from Holly Lane to Alcott Lane just before the war.

2009 The modern 'Tavern' which was built to the left of the older building. The trees have survived, on the 1910 photograph you can see by the seating outside the pub that the trees came within the drinking area of the customers along with the cars. The other hostelry in the village was 'Ye Olde Belle', over 300 years old it was built in 1668 in the reign of Charles II. The main section of the building has not changed over the years, until a modern lounge and car park was added in the 1950s.

1900 'Ye Olde Belle' at the turn of the century. 1910 A strange photograph for a public house – no one is drinking, and the front door appears to be closed one might assume they are all waiting for 'opening time'. There appear to be two youngsters on the left and most of the ladies appear to be smartly dressed. Maybe, because of the children they had arrived early so that they could sit outside, and perhaps in those days 'ladies' did not go into public houses. The licensee's name above the door was Samuel Stephen Plant. The original distinctive sign above the door was taken down in the late 1980s, sadly, and replaced by a mundane sign which simply stated 'The Bell'.

1920 Another old photo' of 'Ye Olde Belle'. The external buildings in the background nearer to the village disappeared in the early 1930s. An interesting point for those with discerning 'taste buds', it was not 'Mitchells and Butlers' in those days, and the notice positioned on the roof between the two windows stated 'Ansells'.

1935 With old buildings demolished, 'Tea Gardens' were provided and the wooden chalet in the distance used to provide teas and ices. Note the 'Midland Red' bus timetable on the left, the return fare to Birmingham was 5 pence in old money, 6 pence from village.

2008 Present day 'The Bell' showing the extensions that have been added post war and the car park which was extended to the rear. As recently as the 1950s there were three cottages at the rear of the car park called 'Bell Cottages' – the Digby Estate literature indicated that they had "ample living accommodation, with outbuildings and water from Birmingham Mains". The 1923 occupants were Richard Linforth and J.J.Bracewell with the third one empty. The tenants were on a monthly rental for an annual charge of £7.16s (£7.80p). At the time that they were demolished the cottage nearest the roadway a gentleman named Read had a sweet shop and in the far end cottage a family by the name of Reynolds lived there.

1970 'The Malt House' built by 'Ansells' about 1960 on the corner of St.Giles Road and Tile Cross Road. It didn't last long and was closed in the 1980s. In the background were a row of three storied apartments which were also demolished.

The 'Malt House' has been replaced by 'St.Giles Care Home' whilst at the present time new apartments are being erected where the early ones in St.Giles Road stood.

Whilst not strictly in the village there was a public house on the A45 which stood beyond the flyover at Stonebridge and was logically called 'The Stonebridge Hotel'.

1920 'The Stonebridge Hotel' on the banks of the River Blythe. The 'Stonebridge Hotel' was said to be more than 200 years old and was always a popular spot for cyclists and motor cyclists for many years, particularly at weekends. It was under threat in the 1960s when it was decided to avoid the long established route through the village of Meriden and the notorious climb up to the 'Triumph' motor cycle works, which in winter months was, to say the least 'hazardous'. The A45 to Coventry was straightened and turned into dual carriageway. During this work it was noticed that the River Blythe was washing away the bank under the footings of the hotel. So even before health and safety was ever thought of, it was demolished.

1948 The popular 'Cock Inn' had to be demolished to meet the demands of Birmingham Airport for longer runways and improved access amenities.

It was located close to the end of Elmdon Lane which followed the southern boundary of the old Elmdon Airport, to where it met the A45 Coventry Road.

At the other end of the village, still standing, is another old pub, the 'White Hart' standing at the junction of East Meadway/Gressel Lane facing Tile Cross Road. Again, like the 'Bell Inn', it has retained its old worldly features.

Chapter 12

AROUND THE VILLAGE

1910 Coleshill Road looking
away from the village.

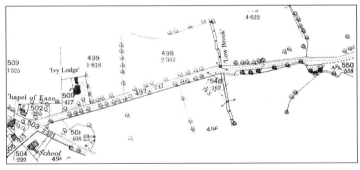

The 1880 Ordnance
Survey Map shows 'Ivy
Lodge' was the only
building on the road from
the Station Road/Land
Lane cross road until you
reach 'Gorse Farm'.

2009 'Ivy Lodge' was the 'convalescent home' for
the 'Cottage Homes' which were opened in 1878.

1910 Coleshill Road looking towards the village.

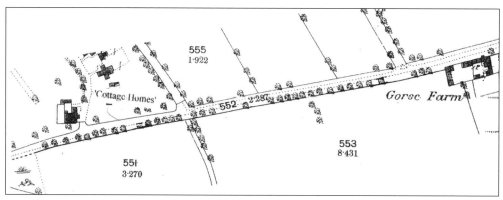

2009 'Gorse Farm'.

1900 An early bridge in Bickenhill Road. The notices gave warnings of potential flooding. There were only three cottages in the entire length of Bickenhill Road and 'Heath Cottage' and 'The Heath' are the only two that have survived. 'Barnett's Cottage' was the home of Miss Barnett the first Head Mistress of the school and was replaced by the family at the present building called 'The Pines'.

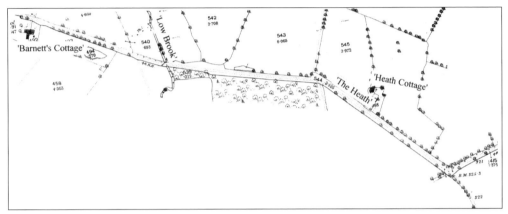

2009 The Bickenhill Road bridge at 'Low Brook'.

1995 Four pairs of semi-detached houses at the far end of Bickenhill Road which were built in 1905. Numbering of houses came to Marston Green in 1933 but despite several attempts by the occupants of these houses to be numbered like the rest of the village, the requests were turned down or ignored over the years. All eight houses have individual names to their houses from the village end 'Sunnyside', 'Oakamoor', 'Jesmondene', 'Longfield', 'Elleburn', 'Burwood', 'The Coppice' to 'Portmans' at the far end.

In the 1911 Census the first known occupants of individual houses were 'Sunnyside' Thomas Fitter Onley aged 36, his wife Alice Mary aged 44 and their son Eric Thomas Onley 4. 'Longfield' – Clement Arton aged 42, his wife Elsie Eleanor aged 39, their son Clement Hugh aged 3 and a servant Elsie Hawkins. 'Elleburn' – Benjamin William Goode aged 51, his wife Ellen Sarah aged 39 and a servant Harriet Jesson. 'Burwood' – Alfred Henry Bishton aged 24 and his wife Elsie Emma aged 24, 'The Coppice' – William Henry Heath aged 40, his wife Alice May aged 26, their son Henry William aged 1, daughter Sheila Mary aged 7 months and servant Elizabeth Parsons. 'Portmans' – Charles David Eaton aged 52, housekeeper Blanche Weston aged 47, widow Mary Cox aged 71 and servant Annie Salisbury.

Later on Eddie Griffin and his wife Jean (nee Chance) lived at 'Sunnyside', Thomas Marks and his family lived at 'Longfield', Paul and Enid Clark and family lived at 'Burwood', William Rogers and family lived at 'The Coppice' and the Seymour family lived at 'Portmans'. On querying the number of 'servants' in those early days I was told by a current occupier that all the houses were built with servants in mind and every house had a 'bell push call' fitted to each room.

Across the road three other properties were built in 1910. 'East Woodhay' the home of Walter Bulpitt and his wife for many years. Whilst their home was being built they were believed to have occupied 'Heath Cottage'. The two bungalows lower down named 'Sherrington' and 'Rosemary' were added later.

The Bulpitts bought much of the land around 'East Woodhay' down to the 'Low Brook', each side of the 'Donkey Path' and the wooded area of 'School Rough'. The 'Bulpitt Estate' still exists although 'East Woodhay' was sold and is now a guest house with 10 bedrooms, 'School Rough' remains as a conservation area.

2009 'East Woodhay' the home of the 'Bulpitt' family for over 60 years. The 'Bulpitts' were an established company founded in the 1800s known as 'Swan Brand' kitchenware. During the war years they made armaments for the Royal Navy and the Army. Walter Henry Bulpitt was the eldest son of Walter Bulpitt who was a 'Master' Tin Plate worker. Walter Henry Bulpitt married a neighbour from the Yardley area, Harriet Viney at Yardley Old Church. When they moved to Marston Green they lived in a house opposite to 'East Woodhay' whilst the house was built in 1909. They are listed in the 1911 Census as Walter Henry aged 30, Harriet Ann aged 30, and a servant Winifred Mary Barley. They had three children, Maurice born in 1910, Francis born in 1912 and Patricia born in 1917. The three children grew up and went to a 'Dame' school in the village hall with Mrs. Coleman, the Vicar's wife.

2008 'Sherrington' at the far end of Bickenhill Road.

'Rosemary' was built later than 'East Woodhay' by Albert Bulpitt, the younger brother of Walter Henry Bulpitt. He lived there for a number of years but then moved to Hampton in Arden. The Austin family followed at 'Sherrington' and with two sons, the father ran a model steam train on a 3½ gauge track in the garden which was much enjoyed by the boys and their friends. After them came the Codrington family who were there until the 1960s.

2008 'Rosemary' at the far end of Bickenhill Road. Probably built at about the same time as the adjoining house next door. Neither of the two houses were built in time to be listed in the 1911 Census.

At the rear of 'East Woodhay' on the area known as 'School Rough' there were only two buildings shown on the 1880 Ordnance Survey Map, a small cottage called 'Shangri La' and a four bedroomed cottage called 'Oakview Cottage'. But not shown was a large wooden 'chalet' and an open fronted 'long barn'.

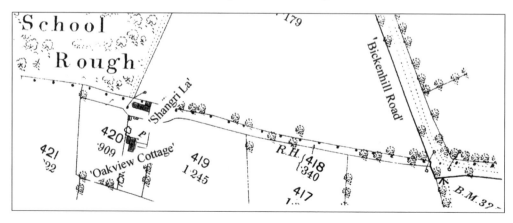

'Shangri La'.

'Oakview Cottage'.

In the 1881 Census there was only one family listed the 'Adams' family – Thomas Adams aged 62, his wife Sarah aged 65, son Frederick 25, daughter Elizabeth 22 and a 'boarder' Mary Banks. They would have lived in 'Oakview Cottage' as 'Shangri La' could not have housed five people. In the next Census of 1901 there were two families listed. John Lovegrove aged 43, his wife Ellen aged 30, and three boys, John aged 10, William aged 8 and Edward aged 4. They would have been in 'Oakview Cottage' and in 'Shangri La' were another 'Adams' family, Henry Adams aged 57, his wife Hannah aged 61 and daughter Myra aged 21. Myra was listed as a schoolteacher. It has been documented elsewhere that a 'DAME' school had at some time been at School Rough. It was logical that Myra had been the teacher. The Education Act came into being in 1870 and it is known that several 'DAME' schools did operate locally before that date. 'Dame' schools were introduced in 1649 and the name indicated that they had a female head teacher. In the 1911 Census, Myra had moved on but Henry and his wife were still there, some 10 years older.

2009 'Oakview Cottage'.

By the time we get into pre-war days, the School Rough 'wooden chalet' was occupied by Herbert Perkins, his wife and two daughters, Peggy and Betty. Samuel Rawlins, and family arrived in 1931, Jessie his wife and their children, daughter Mabel aged 17 at the time, sons Alfred aged 14 and

Jack 12. The family lived in 'Oakview Cottage'. Jack Rawlins and his wife Rene now live in Lyndon Croft and he has just celebrated his 90th birthday. In 1933 Wilfred Webb and his wife Annie came to the village with their daughter Vera and they lived in 'Shangri La'. Vera now lives in Elmdon Road.

Right up to the present day, the cottage has in recent years been modernised by the present owners Robert and Mary Watson. 'Shangri La' is lived in by a Mr. Grimes. There is however a new bungalow called 'Holly Lodge' which is built on what was once part of the garden of 'Oakview Cottage'. The present owners are long term residents of Marston Green, Brian and Barbara Longstaffe who moved into the new bungalow some 7 years ago. There has been a new development built where the old Chalet used to be of three properties which are at the moment available for letting.

2009 'Holly Lodge'.

2009 The 'Long Barn' probably some 300 years old. Has recently been turned into living accommodation with a view to letting. It lies on the right just past 'Shangri La'.

2009 The new accommodation at 'School Rough' which has replaced the old 'chalet' which was until recently the home of George and Gwen Brown.

1928 Holly Lane – the shop on the immediate left was called 'Station Stores' when it was just a sweet shop owned by William Duke who also owned and operated a Timber Yard and Sawmill at the rear of the premises. The property in those days was divided into two units, on the left hand side there was an early Telephone Exchange in a room at the rear, whilst the front room was used as a 'twice a week surgery' for a Doctor Cant from Coleshill. Later a gentleman by the name of Holder bought the premises and installed his sister 'Hetty' to manage the sweet shop. The shop on the other side of the road with the sun blind was the 'Chelmsley Drug Store' owned by Mrs. Louisa Bates who not only acted as Pharmacist but for a few years accommodated the village Post Office there.

1930 Station Road was a single carriageway leading into the village, chimneys to the left were those of the old 'Tavern' and the building beyond was 'Griffin's Garage'. Original 'Wrensons' grocery store in Station Road.

The building in 1910 was a private grocery store owned by a gentleman named 'Croad'. At some time about 1920, he sold out to a midland multiple grocery company called 'Wrensons'. Mr. Cochran was the first Manager and he remained there until 1928 when my father Edmund Crawford followed him as Manager.

However, my father did not stop with 'Wrensons' too long as in 1930 he bought the premises mentioned earlier, the 'Chelmsley Drug Store' in Holly Lane and opened a rival Grocery and Greengrocery business there.

Harry Haines replaced my father as Manager and he remained there until the closure of 'Wrensons' in the 1990s. The Haines family had three sons Robert, Keith and Alan. In the photograph seen through the gap alongside the store was 'High Elm Farm' which disappeared in the late 1930s to make way for Elm Farm Avenue which came as a result of the notice in the hedge which indicated the land was for sale. The magnificent tree was a target for all youngsters in the autumn (including me) as the tree was the finest chestnut 'conker tree' in the village.

1997 The present day 'Flair' sign board removed by high winds resulting in the original 'Croad' visible again, some 80 years after it was first erected.

The enclosure in the village now known as the 'Memorial Garden' was a water filled hollow referred to by locals as 'The Pit' which had been excavated for gravel to improve the tracks that ran from farm to farm throughout the village. Old inhabitants of years gone by, used to recall that the 'Pit' was well stocked with fish, and in dry summers they used to rescue the fish, and keep them in water butts until the rains returned.

Apparently, at the turn of the 19th Century , the level of the water in the 'Pit' used to rise up to road level which poured over Station Road and Elmdon Road and the fish had to be rescued again. The problem was resolved by the building of the 'Cottage Homes' and the sinking of an 'Artesian Well' in 1908. The level of the water dropped dramatically overnight and the 'Pit' has never overflowed since. The Artesian Well provided the water needed for cooling purposes in the hospital Power Station and Boiler Houses. It is still there, what it is used for these days I have no idea, but it is known that with all the building that has gone on in recent years, 'Chelmsley Wood', 'Wavers Marston' etc, the water table has lowered considerably.

1920 to 1940 was a significant period in the past of Marston Green, in those early days modern housing came to the village. Similarly, businesses and a variety of shops were built mainly in the areas along Station Road.

1950 The houses in Station Road which were demolished were No.38 occupied by the 'Hodnett' family called 'Wayside'. The two semi-detached houses were 'Belmont House' and 'Stockton House' homes of the 'Ivers' and 'Johnson' families. Earlier the 'Harrow' and 'Ellis' families lived there. The detached house beyond was occupied by the 'Hallam' family and quite recently John and Daphne Halton lived there.

2009 The new 'Wayside' – development of 34 houses which replaced the three demolished houses, and was erected off Station Road and to the rear of No.46 on the right of the photograph, which was built at the same time.

For many years prior to the war a feature in the village was the old 'Gravel Pit' which had been excavated at the time gravel was needed for the roads in the village which had, probably up to the 1880s been rough tracks.

1925 The 'Gravel Pit' between Station Road and Elmdon Road. In the background is the old St.Leonard's Church and the building to the right with a sign on the wall is No.2 'The Cottage' in Land Lane, an early Post Office. The pool was popular in summer months and children used to paddle there and bring their nets along to catch the fish. Similarly, everyone enjoyed skating there in winter months. The 'Pit' was finally filled in about 1935 and during the war years, a fabricated Fire Station was erected and villagers formed a volunteer 'Auxiliary Fire Service' team.

The earliest modern building took place in Marston Green in 1870 when 'Prospect Villas' was erected in Elmdon Road and it was recorded in local history that "these buildings were the first to be erected not having any agricultural affinity". At the time that Prospect Villas was built there was an old timber framed cottage opposite, occupied by an old soldier with long service in India. He called his dwelling 'Indy' and his garden, lawns and hedges were immaculate and his pride and joy. Apparently it was woe betide any youngster who dared to set foot on his lawn.

In the 1881 Census the occupants of Prospect Villas were listed as George Hill aged 54 an accountant, his wife Hannah aged 59, their sons Arthur 25, Charles 24, both classified as 'Clerk – unemployed' and Alfred 23 who was listed as 'Invalid', and daughters Frances 19 and Caroline 17, both scholars. A second family were William Perkins aged 59 a retired upholsterer, his wife Amelia also 59 and their daughters Elizabeth 22 and Rachel 20. On the same Census there was a retired Army pensioner, John Gee aged 59 who also appeared in the 1901 Census aged 79, could he be the old soldier who lived at the wooden cottage 'Indy'?

Emily Catherine Hall who was a nurse there during the war was a local girl, and was shown on the 1901 Census as living on 'Malt House Farm' aged 2 years, the grand daughter of Edward Hall aged 84, the retired farmer at Malt House Farm. At that time the farm was managed by Richard aged 37 (the son of Edward), his wife Elizabeth aged 33, with their children Edward aged 4 , Emily mentioned above and baby Francis just 3 months old.

1920 'Prospect Villas' in Elmdon Road used as a hospital in the 1914/1918 War.

2009 Modern day 'Prospect Villas'.

On appearances the properties do not seem to have changed structurally since the earlier photograph was taken. The large chimney on the right has been reduced in height and old trees have been removed. No.35, the right hand property does look the same as 1870, but significant changes have been made to No.37. Whilst the

1945 The 'old' Village Hall opposite 'Prospect Villas' in Elmdon Road.

When V.E. (Victory in Europe) arrived a large bonfire Celebration took place in the village, individual street parties took place and, left, the village children attended an open air party at the old Village Hall.

frontage has been retained there are 3 self contained flats at the rear numbered 37a, 37b and 37c. There is a private Car Park at the rear of No.37.

Most roads in the village in the 1920s evolved generally around the farms and cottages, no effective surfaces, no pavements, no road drainage and no street lighting. Elmdon Lane was no different – but probably less accessible.

The photograph shows the corner where Elmdon Road met Elmdon Lane. This point does look as though this was the end of the Lane but in fact there was access from this point which continued for almost two miles to join the Birmingham to Stonebridge Turnpike Road (A45) as it was called then. An earlier booklet 'Discovering Bickenhill' refers to the 1774-75 Act which was passed to 'repair the road from Birmingham to

1920 Elmdon Lane before the houses came.

Stonebridge' because its 'so ruinous … that coaches cannot pass without damage'. A 'toll' was introduced but local agricultural traffic was exempt.

Tolls were further increased in 1788 when the turnpike was widened and its course altered. In 1826 the turnpike was classified as third class. The turnpike by 1835 was part of Telford's famous Holyhead Road between London, the north west and Dublin and carrying mail to Yarmouth. The turnpike continued a precarious existence for the next 34 years. Tolls in 1869 brought in only £637 and the Trust was £336 in debt. Sounds like our M6 Toll road! However, by 1872 all debts were paid, the road was 'disturnpiked' and the Poll Trust dissolved.

Crossing the Elmdon Road railway bridge, which was known apparently as 'Whitmore's Bridge' (I do not know who he was), there were a row of 6 terraced houses which it is believed were built in the early 1900s. Rightly or wrongly, the houses were known by locals as 'Mellish's'. In the 1901 Census there was a George A.J.Mellish aged 32 trading as a Coal Merchant, his wife was named Mary aged 33, and at the time they had two sons Frederick aged 4 and Henry aged 2. It does seem logical that George Mellish could well have had those houses built.

In the latest 1911 Census, George and Mary Mellish and family were still listed again, with their sons being at school. Henry however then calling himself Harry. There were, however, additions to the family with two nieces, Bessie Mellish aged 19 a dressmaker, and May Mellish aged 17 a Clerk, and a nephew Albert White aged 5.

In pre-war days before midwives became available there, was a 'maternity bag' which Mary Mellish looked after. In the bag were sheets, towels, nightdresses and baby clothes. This bag was for use as and when any villager had a baby, the bag was loaned to the family temporarily, and then returned to Mrs. Mellish who restocked the bag as necessary.

Sadly, Frederick the eldest son lost his life in the First World War. Years later, Harry Mellish and his family lived in the same house, with their two daughters Doreen and Shirley. Harry continued with the family business for many years into the 1960s. Today, daughter Shirley Mellish still lives there.

2009 The six early terraced houses in Elmdon Road, there are four other semi-detached houses beyond but they arrived later probably about 1925 when other houses arrived in Elmdon Lane.

1930 Early properties and bungalows looking towards the village at the far end of Elmdon Lane. The houses on the left had individual names but nowadays are numbered from 188 onwards. Electric poles to carry services to the individual houses were evident and there was also a telephone supply pole in view.

Circa 1928 with early properties in Elmdon Lane looking down to the Elmdon Road corner. The houses were of individual and varied design, with semi-detached, detached 4 bedroomed properties, and 4 bedroomed bungalows. The first semi-detached building on the right nowadays is numbered 120 and 122. Like other roads in the village at that time there were no pavements, no street lighting, the houses had individual names, and tarmac did not arrive in the village until the early 1930s. A local builder George Foster built several of the houses in the photograph.

1995 Taken more or less from the same point. The sloping roof on the right is a dormer bungalow. The double fronted property with the caravan is No.116 and the semi-detached houses numbered 120 and 122 on the earlier photograph are partially hidden by the trees. A bungalow roof, No.18 can be seen between the two properties above, but did not appear to be there on the earlier photograph. The trees are probably at least 50 years old.

2009 No.50 Chelmsley Lane at the junction with Wood Lane. Building date not certain but probably about 1925. The 'Clare' family were early owners of the property and they were followed by 'Peter Kellie' and family who lived there for some 50 years. A recent planning application to demolish the garage and build 2 new properties has been approved.

Chapter 13

MARSTON GREEN HOSPITALS

THE ISOLATION HOSPITAL

In the early 1900s it became law that every village had to have access to an Isolation Hospital. To meet this requirement a fabricated building was positioned away from the village at the bottom of Elmdon Lane on the left hand side beyond the houses. Elmdon Lane at that time continued for some 2 miles and joined the Coventry Road close to the 'Cock Inn' which stood there for many years.

The building was made of corrugated iron sheets and was generally known as the 'Tin Hospital'. There was a small wooden building alongside where a caretaker lived. The lady who lived there used to carry out dressmaking as a part time activity as she did not have much to occupy her time as a caretaker.

Leah Martin was actually taken into the hospital and shown around on one occasion, and in her words it was "like the old hospital programmes you see on television – it had 6 iron beds with white marsella quilts on them, with a 'jerry' under each bed". There was also a wash basin with a large jug rather like the pre-war B & B boarding houses.

Mrs. Martin also remembered that on one occasion two men slept in the hospital for a few days in an emergency, but she couldn't remember what the emergency was.

The hospital was eventually demolished during the war years after some 45 years, but in all that time it was never used as an Isolation Hospital and was superseded by the Catherine de Barnes Hospital after the war. The caretaker moved to a cottage on the other side of the Airport and lived there until well into her 90s.

THE CANADIAN GENERAL HOSPITAL

In 1940 an event took place in Marston Green which was to affect the village not only in the war but for many years after. In that year the No.1 Canadian General Hospital was built on land adjacent to the old 'Cottage Homes'. Intended to treat military casualties, quite ironically in view of what transpired later, the first patients were sick babies evacuated from the Birmingham hospitals, and children injured from the Coventry blitz.

The Chaplain was Father Bill Casson of the Royal Canadian Army Medical Corps.

The hospital consisted of sixteen ward huts around an oval parade ground. The cyclist was Earl Hann who photographed his fellow Canadians during their time in the hospital.

Madeleine Taylor (nee Moulds) recalled the day that the Canadians arrived in the village by train. She indicated that "they formed up in line and marched in formation through the village and we were all most impressed. Many of the local people invited them into their homes and Mother (Amy Taylor) often invited a Canadian named Frank into our home for meals and we became good friends".

1941 The Canadian Medical Corps pipe band took part in Marston Green's War Weapons Week parade. Most of these men were originally from Scotland, and worked for Sun Life Assurance in Montreal before the start of the war.

October 1941 A visit by the local Marston Green A.R.P. (Air Raid Precautions) members. Later the Canadian Medical Corps followed the Allies into mainland Europe and had distinguished service during the invasion of Italy in 1943.

There is some confusion over the date when baseball was introduced to Marston Green. The original diamond was in fact laid out by Durex Abrasives before the war on private land.

Maple Leafs History is brought to you by our primary sponsor Midlaw Legal Services

MAPLE LEAFS ORGANISATION HISTORY

The Beginnings Of Birmingham Baseball

Much like many Major League teams of the United States the Maple Leafs and its organisation are blessed with a rich and engaging history.

Unsurprisingly the teams players and organisers pride themselves in knowing the part they play in a continuing legacy that dates back over sixty baseball years makes them virtually unique in UK amateur baseball.

The first era of Marston Green baseball history began in the World War II summer of 1940, when the British government sequestered many hospitals around the country for the purpose of providing commonwealth allies with suitable facilities to care for there war casualties. Marston Green's Hospital was one such hospital allocated to the allies. More Specifically the Royal Canadian Medical Corp. The Corp occupied Marston Green Hospital for a five-year period, and in that time Canadian casualties were frequently transferred for medical attention to hospital #7, as it was then known. During their convalescence the patients frequently participated in recreational activities on the hospital grounds, which are now known as Marston Green Recreation Ground. The main activity for the Canadian casualties was obviously baseball, as ice hockey rinks were not widely available in wartime Marston Green. Due to this lack of ice the Maple Leafs legacy was born and the bats were swung with regularity throughout the war on the make shift diamond that was marked out by the Canadian servicemen. Once the war was won and the surviving servicemen made their long journey home, the diamond lay dormant until the new millennium. Overgrown but still clearly visible the diamond was reawakened in 2003 by a baseball enthusiast who was totally enthralled by the grounds enchanting history. 63 years after the first bat was swung the second era of Marston Green baseball History began, with the help of one baseball enthusiast who set out on a quest to rekindle the flame of the grounds former glories.

It does seem that the current Maple Leaf organisation do not know the geographical difference between Marston Green of wartime and present day Marston Green. This leaflet clearly states that the 'patients frequently participated in recreational activities on the hospital grounds, now known as Marston Green Recreation Ground' and that wartime baseball was played on a 'makeshift diamond'.

This ignores the fact that the hospital grounds where their baseball diamond was situated, and the Marston Green Recreation Ground which has been there since 1937, were at least half a mile apart. The second statement states 'the diamond lay dormant until the new millennium' is again not quite true. They have 'discovered' the diamond which was laid before the war by Durex Abrasives which was on private land and obviously they have not appreciated that this diamond is not the hospital diamond. I have written to the Maple leafs but they have never replied, probably because they prefer to believe that they have 'rekindled the flame of the grounds former glories', and are 'enthralled by the grounds enchanting history'.

MARSTON GREEN MATERNITY HOSPITAL

Marston Green Maternity Hospital came into being in September 1948 when the former Canadian Hospital off Berwicks Lane closed and the premises were handed over to the health service. It was recorded that the first baby born there was to a lady from Kingstanding with the name of Smith.

In the 44 years of the hospitals service, apparently some 3000 babies were regularly delivered each year and quite remarkably in 1960 they achieved a claim to fame when they entered the 'Guinness Book of Records' as having the most births during the year, when in excess of over 6,500 babies were born there.

However, on 26th October 1992, sadly to many residents of Marston Green and neighbouring areas, the hospital closed for the last time. It is known that many residents have seen their children born there, their grandchildren and in some cases even their great-grandchildren born there. Amongst the last patients on that day were Mrs. Patricia Lewis and Mrs. Joan Clark both from Castle Bromwich, Mrs. Evelyne Tomlinson from Chelmsley Wood and Mrs. Noreen Pitt from Pype Hayes. Sister Nash who was on duty emphasised, that although the building itself was closing, the actual unit was moving with most of the staff to East Birmingham Hospital ('Heartlands'), where treatment and admissions would carry on as normal.

Mrs. Lucille Green, who at present is Vice Chair of Bickenhill Parish Council, came to Marston Green from Chester in 1968 to commence midwifery training at the Maternity Hospital. In an article she wrote for the 40th Anniversary of the Marston Green Library, she recalled her disappointment when she arrived and her feelings that the hospital was more of a 'military barracks', which of course it had been as the former Canadian Hospital during the war years.

Wards A to P were connected by a covered walkway which was referred to as 'The Horse Shoe' due to the layout of the hospital buildings, which opened out to a garden full of rose trees and bushes. She pointed out that due to the rural location of the hospital with public transport amounting to one bus per hour, the hospital had its own transport vehicle (which was fondly known as the 'Agony Wagon'), and enabled patients from all over Birmingham to attend hospital clinic appointments.

The same vehicle was used to transport pupil midwives to East Birmingham Hospital for lectures, and for nurses to attend church services on Sundays.

She pointed out that the hospital was noted as being the largest Maternity Hospital in the country. Another claim to fame occurred when Ozzy Osborne was born there in 1948. Marston Green Maternity Hospital had an excellent reputation as a teaching hospital, attracting nurses from all over the world to train as midwives. Once qualified, midwives were proud to wear the hospital badge which represented a 'maple leaf' in tribute to the Canadians.

Lucille had memories of the Matron, Miss Minyrey Maxwell M.B.E. who was a highly respected formidable figure who 'ran a tight ship'. She was passionate not only for the well being of the nurses and babies but also of the hospital staff. She ensured that hot meals were available at all times, and if staff were ill, arrangements would be made for their comfort.

Because of the rural environment of the hospital, it became a very close knit unit. A variety of entertainments were arranged, and Miss Maxwell made sure that the hospital maintained strong links with the village community.

Villagers were invited to many social activities, such as parties, garden fetes, musical evenings and the annual pantomimes. Many of the 'ugly sisters' or 'pantomime dames' went on to become respected G.P.s and consultants.

Lucille's own personal memory of these functions which she especially remembered was the fact that she met her husband at one of the functions.

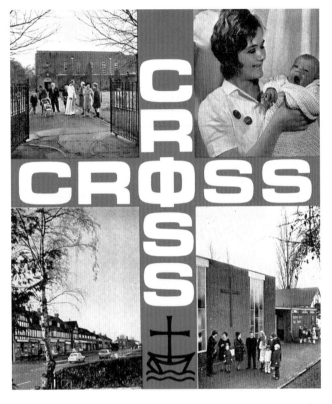

She recalled one occasion when the Matron summoned her to the Office. I was informed that a local photographer was waiting to take her photograph. This was needed for a fresh front cover for the local church magazine of 'Criss Cross'.

Four photographs were to be taken to represent Marston Green. The village shops, the two churches and one to relate to the Maternity Hospital.

For interest in the pictures of the two churches, the Vicar at St. Leonard's at that time was Rev. Michael H. Zair and the Minister at the Free Church was Rev. Peter M. Goodall. In the magazine with those photographs it gave notice that on Wednesday 8th September 1971, Matron Miss Maxwell was to hold in her flat a session of "Coffee in the morning, coffee in the evening and tea in the afternoon".

For information, it made the formal announcement that Mr. Paul Raymer had agreed to take on the job of Editor of 'Criss Cross'. By the time that you read this article Paul will have reached the 38th Anniversary of his Editorship – congratulations to him.

In the photograph over the page Miss Maxwell, on the left, is showing the Lady Mayoress of Solihull some of the linen ware, baby woollen clothing and knitted items produced by the ladies present, whom I believe called themselves the 'Maternity Linen League' or similar. They also prepared embroidered cot covers and blankets for babies at the Maternity Hospital.

1958 Lady Mayoress of Solihull attending what is believed to be the 10th Anniversary of the Maternity Hospital opening.

Quite a 'family gathering' as immediately behind the Mayoress's party was my grandmother Emily King, my wife Joan Crawford and my mother Winifred Crawford. The two ladies beyond my mother were Mrs. Anne Minnie, sister of Frank Walcott, Councillor and local shopkeeper, and Miss Nancy Robson, his housekeeper.

Chapter 14

ELMDON AIRPORT

WHILST SIGNIFICANT development of new housing increased in Marston Green following the 'break up' of the 'Digby Estate' in the early 1920s, it was simultaneously followed and continued into the 1930s with many commercial activities mainly of retail shop outlets. There was however, other activities being contemplated which would forever change the image of Marston Green as a farming village community.

These included an 18 hole golf course, a Cinema to be called the 'Clifton' but more disturbing at the time, a municipal airport to serve the City of Birmingham. This 'later' project was submitted to the local authorities as early as 1928, but financial shortcomings at that time prevented further progress until 1934. After this passage of time it had been agreed that the optimum site would be at Elmdon. This obviously raised tremendous criticism from numerous sources with Bickenhill Parish Council being at the forefront of these objections.

The first tentative figures quoted, indicated that 300 acres would be required for the Airport, but after much arguing and debate it was decided that further land was required. Compulsory purchase orders were issued and a further 200 acres were obtained. Finally in 1935 approval was given to the new Airport work started immediately. The 'Cock Inn' on the Coventry Road and two farms 'Elmdon Farm' and 'Newlands' disappeared. Hundreds of trees and hedges were removed, levelling of the site was carried out over the whole of the area and some 40 miles of drainage provided.

The opening ceremony of 'Elmdon Airport' was performed by H.R.H. the Duchess of Kent in July 1939 which, unfortunately, was rather spoiled by incessant rain more or less all day long. The day before had been glorious sunshine and I was taken by my father on a 10 shilling (50p) flight in a De Havilland 'Rapide' cabin plane of the King's Flight.

The cost of the Airport was reported as £360,000 but at the time of the opening only a quarter of the compulsory land purchase was in use. The runways were grass and there were three shorter strips and a main runway of 4,700 feet.

At the time of the Airport opening, Elmdon Lane ran round the southern perimeter boundary reaching the A45 Coventry Road near to the 'Cock Inn'. There

The new Terminal Building of Elmdon Airport 1939.

was no reason that this direct route from Marston Green to the Coventry Road would not remain open. But two months after the opening ceremony war was declared.

The Airport was taken over and transferred to the Ministry of Defence and Elmdon was used as a training ground for R.A.F. and Fleet Air Arm Pilots. The favoured aircraft for this exercise were 'Tiger Moth' biplanes. Within weeks following the start of the war a 'shadow factory' was under construction in Bickering Lane adjacent to Elmdon Airport sited across the other side of the Birmingham to Coventry railway. Within months this new factory was used for the assembly of Short's 'Stirling' bombers and to accommodate these aircraft for operational duties a wide bridge was built straddling the railway to allow the bombers to be towed across the bridge and on to the Airport.

First Air Liner to land at Elmdon of the Great Western and Southern Air Lines on 1st May 1939.

These proceedings resulted in two separate happenings. Firstly, Elmdon Lane no longer continued to the Coventry Road but more importantly it allowed the main runway to be extended for the 'Stirling' bombers to fly off to war zones mainly in the Mediterranean. The existing grass runways were replaced by two extended hard surface runways. The planes were piloted by a local resident Doug Cotton who played cricket for Marston Green before and during the war years.

After the war the Ministry of Aviation took over and later the City of Birmingham gained control in 1960 and renamed it 'Birmingham International Airport'. Over the next decade demand for larger aircraft saw further runway extensions and the aforementioned golf course was first reduced to 9 holes and then finally disappeared in the early 1970s.

On the Bickenhill Lane side of the railway came the arrival of the giant N.E.C. complex and an overhead Maglev light railway link brought the two activities together in conjunction with the new 'Birmingham International Station'. Events at the N.E.C. brought new passengers for these events from Europe and further afield. Similarly, the arrival of the M42 Motorway gave passage from the M1 and M6 and offered easier access for newer passengers from across the country who wished to use the Airport.

Major companies from the United States, Australasia and the Far East soon began to queue up wanting to use Birmingham Airport. What was at first early flights into European countries soon extended to world wide operations. After such humble beginnings, Elmdon has kept up with the demands for global travel and has achieved acceptance as an international player in the market to offer larger catchment area passengers the opportunity for travel to countries more or less anywhere in the world.

Even now, despite what has been achieved, there are still ongoing demands for a third runway to be able to attract even larger and more powerful aircraft.

The photograph, left, shows the remains of the 6 seater 'Beechcraft Baron' which crashed at Birmingham Airport on Saturday 29th November 1975 at 9.00pm in thick fog after attempting a third 'instruments only' landing. The light aircraft overshot the main runway, crashed through fencing, hit a tree and disintegrated in a field short of the houses in Elmdon Lane. Four people died in the crash, three of them experienced pilots. They were 61 year old Eric Allchin, the owner and pilot, his wife Pamela, Arthur Penzer and Miss Betsy Kidd all from Solihull.

Mr. Penzer, a former RAF pilot was chief flying instructor for Warwickshire Aero Club. Mr. Allchin had been the Club's Pilot of the year in 1973 and 1974. Miss Kidd was also an experienced pilot.

No other aircraft attempted to land at the Airport on that Saturday night. Aircraft scheduled to land were diverted to other airfields by their companies.

Residents from Elmdon Lane heard the crash and ran to the scene. First on the scene were Daniel Jackson and his neighbour Colin Harvey, they stumbled across a body, still alive at the time, the other two men had no pulse or signs of life, and they were unable to reach the woman who was still in the plane.

The Royal opening of the terminal building at Birmingham International Airport 25 years ago..

Silver celebration at airport

To mark the 70th Anniversary of Elmdon Airport's official opening the 'Birmingham Post' printed this earlier cutting of the 25th Anniversary of the opening of the terminal building back in 1984. The Queen was accompanied by the Duke of Edinburgh. The terminal building was completed 12 weeks ahead of schedule and was seen as one of the most modern facilities in the UK and Europe at the time.

September 9th 2009, 70 years after the Airport's first passengers departed in an 8 seater De Havilland 'Rapide' aircraft, today's passengers had the one off opportunity to fly on the largest passenger aircraft ever built, the 'Emirates Airbus A380'.

The flight was the first commercial flight of the 'Airbus' in the UK outside of London, and it was fitting that the aircraft was also the first to use Birmingham International Airport's brand new £45 million International Pier. This building is a three storey building for arriving and departing passengers.

The 'AIRBUS A380' has seating spread over two levels where First Class and Business Class have an 'onboard' lounge. First Class passengers can rest in a flat bed, massage equipped suite having Shower Spa. Economy Class has more generous seats with wider aisles.

'Touch down' at 12.20 pm at Birmingham International Airport.

'Taxiing' to terminal building.

The 'Airbus' departed from Birmingham International Airport and took off from the Sheldon Park end. The photograph shows a typical view of a section of some 500 enthusiastic supporters who gathered there to watch.

'Airbus' approaching the runway for take off.

'Airbus' on runway at moment of take off.

Chapter 15

EVENTS IN
MARSTON GREEN

SILVER JUBILEE OF KING GEORGE V and QUEEN MARY
MAY 6th 1935

A fancy dress parade was held on a 'special' Bank Holiday through the village to commemorate the Jubilee, every child at the village School was encouraged to attend and their parents supported them with a varied and appropriate display of costumes.

Harry Mellish local Coal Merchant, in dark suit on left, Peter Arton – Scoutmaster in foreground, Jean Crawford and Dorrie Thompson alongside. From memory there was a good attendance of Red Indians and several girls dressed as the Queen with suitable headgear to match. Parade is passing what is now the Memorial Garden.

Clarrie Bate – Headmaster of Marston Green School, in flannels and blazer, behind him Mr. A.Thomas the local Gas Fitter with his young daughter. Surprisingly, pavements do not appear to have arrived on either side of the road at that time.

CORONATION OF KING GEORGE VI and QUEEN ELIZABETH
MAY 12th 1937

Fancy dress parade through the village to commemorate the Coronation.

The parade passing the shops in Station Road with shop decorations evident.

Brenda Roberts, June Robinson and Peggy Perkins apparently smoking pipe.

Decorated float from Aston's the Butchers with Eric Brelsford taken in Elmdon Lane, the start point of the parade. There were several decorated floats all belonging to local traders.

Pam Carpenter and Alma Popplewell in front, Brenda Watson with sunshade and Adele Creas on right.

Three generations of the 'Aston' family, Reg the local Butcher with his son George mounted wearing a 'topper', with grandfather Frank smartly attired with his 'bowler'.

Lady Godiva passing the Elmdon Road/Lane crossroads. She didn't seem to be attracting too much attention, though I understand that the earlier version titled lady in Coventry had less clothing on than our version. I notice however, the boy on the bike has his foot on the floor and looking on – was he supposed to be 'peeping' Tom.

Graham Crawford – the Highway Code (Belisha Beacons had just been introduced to the unsuspecting public), with his sister Jean (Miss Ovaltine) and the Girls' winner in her age group.

DEDICATION OF MEMORIAL PLAQUES AT GARDEN OF MEMORY on JULY 17th 1949

Dedication Ceremony, Lord Guernsey on extreme right. Combined choirs from St.Leonard's and Baptist Free Church on the left, and in the background 'old' St.Leonard's Church and 'Ash Tree Cottage'.

Lord Guernsey, later Lord Aylesford unveiling the plaques with Rev. N.W.Buckley from Bromsgrove carrying out the Dedication at the Ceremony. The Guard of Honour were soldiers from the Royal Warwickshire Regiment.

FESTIVAL OF BRITAIN WEEK AUGUST 12th to 18th 1951

The object of the Marston Green Festival Week was to bring together all of the various societies, activities and clubs in the village, to provide a programme of Events, so that everyone in the village participated with a view to appreciate the many voluntary organisations that operate in the village. Part of the profits went to the planting of trees and shrubs in the grass central section of the dual carriageway in Station Road.

'Festival Queen' Elspeth Purdie in centre with her attendants Barbara Hardman on her right, and Doreen Hone on her left, leading the Carnival Procession.

Off to the Festival Parade about to cross Land Lane Railway Bridge. Pauline Huddleston and John Jenkins on the left, Ann Bate on the right with Alan Martin behind her. The open space behind is now occupied by the School football pitch.

FESTIVAL OF BRITAIN WEEK – PROGRAMME OF EVENTS

Programme of Events

SATURDAY, AUGUST 11th.
Tennis Tournament
Play by the Marston Green Players

SUNDAY, AUGUST 12th.
Church Service at the Parish Church
Children's Service at the Free Church

MONDAY, AUGUST 13th.
Model Railway
Play by the Marston Green Players

TUESDAY, AUGUST 14th.
Model Railway
Football Match—Marston Green v. Aston Villa XI
Whist Drive in the Village Hall

WEDNESDAY, AUGUST 15th.
Model Railway
Dance and Crowning of Festival Queen

THURSDAY, AUGUST 16th.
Model Railway
Cricket Match—Cricket Club v. Football Club

SATURDAY, AUGUST 18th.
Carnival Procession
Horticultural Society's Flower Show

President: T. B. WEATHERHOGG, Esq.

Chairman: Mr. J. HAMAR.   Vice-Chairman: Mr. W. KIRKPATRICK.

Hon. Treasurer: Mr. A. STEVENS.

Hon. Secretary: Mr. W. W. HILLING

Committee

Mrs. J. Martin, Mrs. H. Mellish, Mrs. E. Ryder, Messrs. R. F. Aston, A. E. Bourne, T. E. Brelsford, T. R. Burrowes, E. Crawford, J. A. Dooley, G. H. Foster, H. Harvey, E. W. Hayes, E. Howard, W. Knibbs, H. Mellish, R. Moseley, O. Norman, H. Perkins, H. Richards, E. Ryder, F. Stonehouse, H. Storey, W. L. Wright.

Saturday, August 11th, 1951

Marston Green Lawn Tennis Club Mixed American Tournament

On the CLUB GROUND, ELMDON ROAD.

Commencing at 2.30 p.m.

Entrance Fee 2/6.   Draw for Partners.

REFRESHMENTS AVAILABLE FOR PLAYERS at popular prices.

Spectators admitted, 6d. each.

Entries, together with entrance fee, should be sent to:—
Mrs. Bowen, 41, Station Road, or Mr. Wilson, 14, Land Lane, not later than Saturday, August 4th.

The entrance fee will be returned if no play is possible owing to rain.

Saturday, August 11th and Monday, August 13th, 1951

Marston Green Village Club

THE MARSTON GREEN PLAYERS present

" Mountain Air "

A LIGHT COMEDY IN THREE ACTS by Ronald Wilkinson

IN THE VILLAGE HALL, MARSTON GREEN.

Commence at 3.0 p.m.   Admission 2/6 and 1/6.

Seats may be booked at Majors, Elmdon Road.

Sunday, August 12th

A Combined Service of the Parish Church and the Free Church

PARISH CHURCH, ELMDON ROAD

at 11.15 a.m.

Conducted by

THE VICAR, REV. H. R. SPROULE
and the Minister of the Free Church,
REV. S. D. CUTHBERTSON.

Led by the Combined Choirs of both Churches.

A Combined Children's Service

will be held in

THE FREE CHURCH, LAND LANE

at 3.0 p.m.

MONDAY, AUGUST 13th, to THURSDAY, AUGUST 16th.

Marston Green Model Arts & Crafts Club

A MODEL RAILWAY

at GRIFFINS CAR PARK, STATION ROAD

will be on show each evening from 6.0 p.m.

Train Fare for the Return Trip: Adults 4d., Children 2d.

Come and see the Railway built by your own Model Arts and Crafts Club.

Tuesday, August 14th, 1951.

Marston Green A.F.C.

have arranged a

Festival Football Match

AN ASTON VILLA XI
(including 1st Division players)

versus

MARSTON GREEN

at the

Recreation Ground, Bickenhill Road

Referee Mr. H. Ryder (Sheldford).

Kick-off 6.30 p.m.   Collection on the Ground.

Watch notices for details of teams.

A WHIST DRIVE

arranged by the Marston Green Golf Club

will be held in the

VILLAGE HALL

Commence 8 p.m.   Tickets 2/6d. including Refreshments.

Festival Queen

Miss Elspeth Purdie

and her two Attendants

MISS BARBARA HARDMAN and MISS DOREEN BONE

will be present

at all the Festival Events during the Week.

SHE WILL DISTRIBUTE THE PRIZES AT THE WHIST DRIVE AND AT THE DANCE AND ALSO AT THE FLOWER SHOW ON THE DUREX SPORTS GROUND.

Wednesday, August 15th, 1951

Marston Green Women's Institute

present

The Carnival Evening of Festival Week

7.45 p.m. DANCING.

8.30 p.m. GRAND CROWNING OF THE FLORAL QUEEN (Musical)

9.30 p.m. CABARET AND SUPPER.

LUCKY SPOT PRIZES AT INTERVALS.
ANKLE COMPETITION.
Come and enjoy a really good evening.
Admission 2/6d.

Thursday, August 16th, 1951

MARSTON GREEN CRICKET CLUB

have challenged

MARSTON GREEN FOOTBALL CLUB

AT CRICKET

To be held on the

CRICKET GROUND, BICKENHILL ROAD.

Wickets pitched at 6.0 p.m.   Collection on the ground.

Saturday, August 18th, 1951

Marston Green and District Horticultural Society

" 25th Year. Silver Jubilee."

Annual

Flower Show and Gymkhana

on the

DUREX SPORTS GROUND, BICKENHILL ROAD.
(by kind permission of DUREX ABRASIVES LTD.)

Ground open 1.30 p.m.   First Event 2.0 p.m.

Admission 1/6d.
(Children under 15 half price.)

Saturday, August 18th, 1951

1st Marston Green Girl Guides

will perform the following

English Country Dances

Commence 3.0 p.m.

1. THE BUTTERFLY.
2. JENNY PLUCK PEARS.
3. THE BLACK NAG.
4. THE DRESSED SHIP.
5. MAYPOLE DANCE.

FESTIVAL OF BRITAIN WEEK
LIST OF LOCAL ORGANISATIONS, SOCIETIES, CLUBS, ETC.

MERIDEN RURAL DISTRICT COUNCIL
Members for Marston Green
Councillors: F.S.Butler and J.Hamar.

BICKENHILL PARISH COUNCIL MEMBERS
Messrs: F.Allcott, F.S.Butler, B.F.Cockersole,
F.C.Cooper, G.H.Foster, J.Hamar,
H.Mellish and Mrs. L. Martin.

CLERK TO BICKENHILL PARISH COUNCIL
J.D.Mynard, Ennersdale Bungalows,Coleshill

ST.LEONARD'S PARISH CHURCH, MARSTON
GREEN, ST. JOHN'S CHURCH, COOK'S LANE,
TILE CROSS.
Vicar: Rev. H.R.Sproule MA. 'Elm Croft' Coleshill
Heath Road, Marston Green. Tel: MAR 2492.
Services/Social dates in monthly parish magazine.

MARSTON GREEN FREE CHURCH LAND LANE.
Minister: Rev. S.D.Cuthbertson MA. 109, Elmdon
Lane, Marston Green. MAR 2726.
Services and Social activities announced in the
Messenger magazine published monthly.

FREE CHURCH ROOM – STATION ROAD.
Hon.Sec: W.J.T. Yaxley, 'West Down' Coleshill
Road, Marston Green. Tel: MAR 2578.

MARSTON GREEN CRICKET CLUB.
Ground: Bickenhill Road.
Hon.Sec. R.T.Coward, 2, Elm Farm Avenue,
2,Elm Farm Avenue, Marston

MARSTON GREEN FOOTBALL CLUB.
Ground: Bickenhill Road.
Hon. Sec: K.Sugarman, 66 Holly Lane, Marston
Green.Tel: MAR 2587.
Green, Tel: MAR 2587.

FREE CHURCH HALL – LAND LANE.
Hon.Sec: C.K.Driscoll, Land Lane, Marston
Green. MAR:2728.

MARSTON GREEN GIRL GUIDES.
Scout Hut, Elmdon Road, Marston Green
Fridays 6.30.pm.
Captain: Miss S.Heath, 56, Elmdon Lane,
Marston Green.

MARSTON GREEN VILLAGE CLUB. Elmdon Road
Hon.Sec: R.S.Hanson, 108, Elmdon Lane,
Marston Green.
Billiards, Snooker, Dramatics and Girls' Sections
Hon.Sec: A.J.Harwood, 16, Elm Farm Avenue,
Marston Green. Tel: Mar 2486.

MARSTON GREEN AND DISTRICT HORTICULTURAL
SOCIETY.
Hon Sec: W.W.Hilling, 15, Elm Farm Avenue
Marston Green. Tel: MAR 2237.

MARSTON GREEN MODEL ARTS AND CRAFT CLUB
Hon Sec. E.J.Withington, 213, Tile Cross Road,
Marston Green.
Meetings at Council School last Wednesday in month.

MARSTON GREEN PIG CLUB.
Hon.Sec; Mrs. L.Martin, 3 Elmdon Road, Marston.

MARSTON GREEN RABBIT AND POULTRY CLUB
Hon Sec: Mrs. Sproston, Newlands Lane, Marston Green.

MARSTON GREEN RESIDENT'S ASSOCIATION.
Hon Sec: Mr. L.Martin, 196, Elmdon Lane, Marston
Green.

MARSTON GREEN BOY SCOUTS.
Scout Hut Elmdon Road.
A.S.M. W.J.Martin, Elmdon Lane, Marston Green.

MARSTON GREEN TENNIS CLUB
Ground: Elmdon Road.
Hon.Sec: W.Wilson. 14, Land Lane, Marston Green.

MARSTON GREEN UNIONISTS ASSOCIATION.
Hon.Sec: F.C.Cooper, 17, Elmdon Road, Marston Green.

MARSTON GREEN WOMEN'S UNIONISTS
ASSOCIATION.
Hon.Sec: Miss Bird, 'Alistair' Chelmsley Lane, Marston
Green. Tel: MAR 2380.

MARSTON GREEN WOMEN'S INSTITUTE.
Hon.Sec: Mrs. D.A.Cowley, 'St.Ives' Coleshill Road.
Marston Green. Tel: MAR 2366.

MARSTON GREEN VILLAGE HALL.
Hon.Sec: A.J.Harwood, 16, Elm Farm Avenue,
Marston Green. Tel: MAR 2486.

MARSTON GREEN COUNTY SCHOOL.
Land Lane, Marston Green.
Head Teacher: C.Bate.

CORONATION OF QUEEN ELIZABETH II on JUNE 2nd 1953.

A Fancy Dress Parade was held as part of the village celebrations to commemorate the Coronation.

Younger children from the Infant's Class waiting in Elmdon Road at the Land Lane cross roads. The building in the background is 'Ye Olde Village Wine Lodge'.

More children in fancy dress waiting outside the old school in Land Lane. Obviously the young lady in front was the 'Queen of Hearts' with another one behind her, not sure what some of the others represented. But there was a decorated bicycle.

More children waiting by the old school in Land Lane for the parade to start. If memory serves me correct, Coronation Day was cold, windy and wet at times – probably explains why most of the children didn't appear to be too happy.

Jack Wright with his decorated float, off to 'Widdecombe Fair'.

One of the decorated floats representing the 'Wash Ladies from the Laundry'. I am not sure whether this was the last 'Fancy Dress Parade' in the village. It is certainly doubtful, under today's Health and Safety requirements, if it would be allowed to have a group of young girls travelling on the flat open back of a lorry. Not to mention insurance if there was an accident.

More Coronation Celebrations – Lyndon Croft where they were probably Frank Sinatra fans as they did it 'their way'.

Peter Jacobs off to the hunt in his full riding outfit.

Children from Lyndon Croft lining up for their fancy dress photograph.

Watching the 'Punch and Judy' show.

More fancy dress for the 'not so old' age group or was it a 'knobbly knees' competition? A young David Anderton is not taking much notice.

Lyndon Croft Coronation Tea Party held at the Scout Hut. Rene Rawlins on the left, and Margaret Cuthbertson on the right making sure that everyone had a fair share.

Lyndon Croft Ladies' football team, not sure who their opponents were, but this team looked 'formidable'. Known ladies amongst the team, Rene Rawlins, Eileen Gallahar, Kitty Harrow, Betty Talbot and Barbara Crane.

Chapter 16

MARSTON GREEN PLAYERS

THE MARSTON Green Players were a very talented amateur dramatics group who operated from 1925 until 1984 with the 'old' Village Hall as their theatre. In that period of time they produced 141 plays, 1 revue and 1 pantomime. The demolition of the old Village Hall, unfortunately brought about the closure of this very popular dramatics group. The design of the new Village Hall was not suitable for the plays to continue, the stage was too high, there was not sufficient space for adequate stage presentations, or for satisfactory stowage of scenery and furniture and equipment.

Frank Pemberton, former stalwart of the Marston Green Players at the 1963 Flower Show with June Marlow. After the war Frank went professional as an actor and made his name as Frank Barlow (Ken Barlow's father) in the early days of 'Coronation Street'. Sadly, Frank having established himself in the role died prematurely. The 'Barlow' family however still continue with William Roache playing the role of Ken Barlow. Frank, prior to the war, lived in Elmdon Lane at the family home owned by his father also named Frank, and during the war he served in the RAF. He married a local girl Dorothy Goodhall.

A typical presentation which the Village Hall was ideally suited for, with the size of the stage area, a large cast and variations of the basic scenery that needed to be amended and used for many different productions. Cast: Left to right, Les Wright, Dora Yarnall, Les Challenor, Kay Coward, Peggy Driscoll, Ernest Clare, George Cuthbertson, Margaret Kirkpatrick, Joan Randall, Phyliss Clare and Colin Harris.

Cast: Left to right, Les Challenor, June Elsdon, Peggy Driscoll, Ernest Clare, Dora Yarnall, Margaret Kirkpatrick and George Cuthbertson.

The cast of 'Reluctant Heroes'.
Back Row: Frank Hazel, David Martin, Dennis Freeman, Peter Ashbourne, Alan Martin, George Norman and George Cuthbertson.
Front Row: Bill Harvey, Susan Hazel, Sybil Robson, Vera Webb and Donald Blakely.

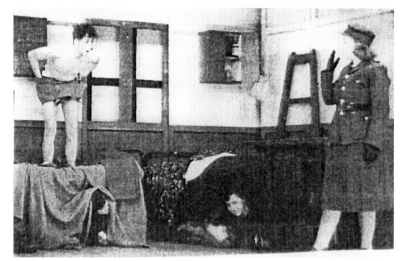

Looks likes a typical Brian Rix 'farce'. Alan Martin on the table having been caught, minus trousers and Sybil Pugh on the right demanding answers to the reason for his state of undress. The young ladies under the tables probably know the answers.

Cast: Left to right, Kay Coward, Vera Webb, George Cuthbertson, June Elsdon, Les Challenor, Peggy Driscoll, Bill Harvey and Margaret Kirkpatrick.

Typical 'pub scene', 3 village ladies putting the world to rights, army sergeant chatting up a local girl, and the pub regulars around the bar.
Cast: Left to right, Kay Coward, Vera Webb, Dora Yarnall, Joan Randall, Bill Harvey, George Cuthbertson, Jimmy Barnett, Dorothy Hankinson, John Gardiner and Alan Martin.

Chapter 17

MARSTON GREEN SCOUTING

1936 Marston Green and Hampton in Arden Scouts at a summer camp at 'Brynbach' in Wales. Peter Arton, the Marston Green Scout Master was 3rd from the left in the rear row and I was in the centre of the front row with the knee length shorts.

Marston Green Scouts at early morning, (before breakfast) 'keep fit and well before 'Aerobics' was in the dictionaries.

1956 Marston Green Scouts and Cubs taken in the Scout Hut.

1965 Marston Green Scouts and Cubs. Taken in the Scout Hut again and co-incidently there are 47 in the group which is the same as 10 years previously. There appears to be more Cubs than before, but it would be interesting to know how many had moved on to Scouting.

1st Marston Green Scout Group

GALA DAY

Saturday 27ᵗʰ June, 2009

in the grounds of St. Leonard's Church, Elmdon Road, Marston Green.

Registered Charity Number 524591

Dear parents,

It's that time of year again! Yes, we're getting ready for **GALA DAY**!

STOP PRESS: The Gala Parade returns!

We are hoping to put last year's disappointment behind us, and bring back the traditional Gala parade around Marston Green. (At the time of writing, we are waiting for the authorities to confirm they will allow us to close the roads for the parade).

As always, we are hoping our main fundraising event of the year will be brilliantly supported by all our member, their families and friends. Equipment and premises have been maintained and updated this year, and we are still aiming to re-roof the HQ.

We've got lots more planned for this year's **GALA DAY**, and we are hoping that as many parents, families and friends of the Scout Group will support us. One of the easiest ways to do so is by helping to sell some of our **GALA DRAW** tickets, not forgetting to buy some yourself!

GALA DRAW 2009

1ˢᵀ PRIZE: IPOD TOUCH 8GB

Together with this letter, your child will bring home 4 books of Gala Draw tickets. We have been supported generously this year by a whole range of businesses, big and small, who have donated some fantastic prizes. These include: Jaffabox, Thinktank, Solihull Ice Rink, Tamworth Castle, Warwick Racecourse and West Midlands Safari Park. We need you to sell some tickets before the Gala itself to friends, neighbours and colleagues. Tickets cost ONLY 20p each, that's £1 for a book of 5!

Please return all ticket stubs and money (**and any unsold tickets**) to your child's Section Leader as soon as possible.

Over the next few weeks we will be asking for volunteers to help make our parade go ahead, as well as donations for various stalls. Look out for letters sent home with the children, and posters on notice boards!

Once again, we'd like to say thank you for your continued support. Funds raised from Gala are essential to keep the Scout Hut roof over our heads, so that your children can continue to take part in all our Scouting and Guiding activities. We need willing volunteers who would like to give us a hand in any way - there are a whole range of ways you could help us to make this year another roaring success! Please speak to a Leader for more information.

The Supporters' Committee

Chapter 18

MARSTON GREEN GIRL GUIDES

1930 An early photograph of Marston Green Girl Guides and Brownies taken outside the 'old' Village Hall where meetings were held in those days.

Another early photograph of Marston Green Girl Guides and Brownies taken in the mid 1930s but the location unknown.

1960s Church Parade, a joint ceremony with the Marston Green Guides, Brownies and the Marston Green Girls' Brigade at St.Leonard's.

Chapter 19

MARSTON GREEN GIRLS' BRIGADE

THE PHOTOGRAPH below, taken in 1970, shows the Mayor of Solihull, Peter Kellie presenting Duke of Edinburgh 'Silver' Award to Susan Bone, with other recipients Elisabeth Clark, Jeanette Crawford and Tessalie Skoczylas on the left.

Also on the photograph are Lady Mayoress, Barbara Kellie and the Girls' Brigade Captain Mrs. Grace Pitman. Pat, Elisabeth, Jeanette and Tessalie went on to receive their 'Gold Awards' which they received from the Duke of Edinburgh at Buckingham Palace. Prior to the ceremony Jimmy Saville gave his own 'version' of the award ceremony which

kept everyone relaxed and minimised nervous tension.

To obtain their 'Gold Award' they were driven to a remote open part of Northamptonshire, given a finishing location, and were given three days to walk some 50 miles distance, using maps to find their way to the destination. This meant that they had to find a route that had convenient

Youth Hostels on the way in order to find sleeping accommodation for two nights. They managed the exercise satisfactorily, and more to the point the weather was good and they enjoyed the experience.

Phone calls from the 4 girls to their parents brought them into the exercise, and gave them the opportunity to show their map reading expertise, by managing to locate their daughters which was again in a remote spot on a canal some way from civilisation.

Chapter 20

THE YOUNGER ELEMENT – LONG AGO

1950 The Girls Section of the Marston Green Club in those days was at the 'old' Village Hall.

Back Row: Mrs. Blizzard, Vera Webb, Margaret Cheshire, Dorothy Hardman, Margaret Hardman, Irene Deeley, Dorothy Weaver, Joan Freeman, Ishbel and Esme Taylor, Barbara Crane and Eileen Gallahar. Seated: Joyce Anderton, Rae Dunford, Eileen Dunford, Mae Gallahar, Alma Popplewell, Kitty Gallahar and extreme right June Elsdon. On the floor, left: Dorrie Thompson, Connie Billington, Gwen Hardman and Jean Chance. On the floor, right: 'Auntie' Peggy Smith (Club Leader), Audrey Green and extreme right Betty Whitehead.

1941 Youth Club members on 'walkabout' looks like the 'Rec'.

Left to right: Harry Musson, Maurice Colloby, Ron Wilson, Edith Ackrill, Joan Freeman, Audrey Green, Brian Jackson, Jack Swindell and Ralf Ludlow.

1942 Youth Club members on a day trip to the 'Clent Hills'. Left to right: Vera Colloby, Irene Deeley, John Harrow, Maurice Colloby, Ron Wilson, Dorothy Weaver and Graham Crawford. Squatting: Paul Shaw and Kitty Gallahar.

1944 21st Birthday Party for Joan Freeman who lived in Elmdon Lane. At rear: Harry Musson and Norman Rollason' Standing: Albert Crook, Joan Freeman, (?) Dorothy Weaver, (?) Vera Webb, Jack Swindell, Irene Deeley and Paul Shaw. Squatting: Betty Whitehead, Jean Chance, Robert Chance, Dora Burton, Eileen Chance and Les Horton.

A much older element – 90th Birthday of Mr. Large.

Mr. Large was the oldest member of the Village Hall Club where he regularly played billiards – he didn't play snooker and he always had difficulty finding someone to play against. Mr. Large married Miss Barnett the first teacher at the village school. Standing: Alf Deeley, Tom Marks, (?) Ted Burton and Bert Hankinson. Seated: Percy Jackson, Mrs. Barnett, Mr. Large, 'Peggie' Smith and Bill Potter.

Chapter 21

TRADESMEN
and SHOPKEEPERS

THE VILLAGE of Marston Green in its early days was basically a farming community, with a population of 302, the Census of 1841 indicated that 187 of them either lived on a farm, or were employed on farms. There were no shops and the villagers had to be self sufficient, the farms were the main suppliers of eggs, poultry, potatoes and other vegetables and if they had a dairy, possibly cheese and butter. Most of the villagers would almost certainly have had their own vegetable garden with fruit trees and might well have their own poultry and even rear pigs. Rabbits were plentiful and villagers would have enjoyed catching rabbits on a regular basis. There was no transport in the village but there were mobile tradesmen, with a butcher being seen on old photographs with a horse drawn cart.

1960 The original workshop of 'Griffins' where they sold and repaired bicycles.

In later years people with capabilities, apart from farming were emerging and amongst those who came to Marston Green in 1919 were a family who previously I believe, had a public house in Corporation Street by the old Fire Station. The family opened up in Station Road as 'Griffins' – repairing and selling bicycles from a wooden workshop, which was situated opposite where the present day 'Wayside' has been since opened up. The motor car had come into vogue, and they moved further into the village and built a Motor Car Garage and Workshop near to the 'Tavern'.

Later the building became a second hand furniture store and a local family named 'Hodnetts' used the premises for some years, but at the time of the photograph it was no longer in use. The driveway is of course the entrance to the 'new' school which had then moved from its Land Lane location where it had been for some 70 years. The large building behind on the right was the local Telephone Exchange. Both of them disappeared shortly after to make way for 'Stephen Henri' a Ladies Hairdressers and extensions to the 'Griffin' Garage with a larger workshop.

1925 The original Garage and Workshop of George Edwin Griffin.

'Griffins' was a family business and George Edwin Griffin had three sons, George, Eddie, Jack and a daughter Leah. Their home was the house on the left of the photograph. The size of the village can be gauged by the telephone number on their advertising board '35'. The fuel pumps were hand

1995 After the Griffins retired there were several changes of ownership, and at this point in time there was a 'Service Centre' on the original location.

operated and the glass tube on the side of the pump had to be 'full' before fuel was pumped into your tank and the price of petrol in those days was 1s 1½d (6p) a gallon.

'James Cycles', 'Pratt's Oils and Petroleum' were advertised on the sign boards. In the 30s and 40s extensions were made and when 'High Elm Farm' was demolished in 1936 they built on the site.

The property remained empty for a few years and the latest occupants of the early garage building was an Estate Agent Company called 'Ferndown Estates' who arrived in 2003. The Griffins house No.30 is now occupied by Mark Davis, Chartered Quantity Surveyor and the property is called 'Island House'. The rest of the workshop was taken over by 'Beauty Revisited' who ran a tanning sauna for ladies, with a variety of other treatments available, facial toning and a massage parlour.

This company did not last very long, probably no more than three or four years and the premises again remained empty.

2009 'U Fit' the latest company who have taken over the original workshop. They supply conservatories, porches, patios, external and indoor doors and a range of tiles and materials available for household conversions.

1995 The forecourt that Griffins built in the 1950s was demolished by the new owners 'Jet'. The pitched roof of the building in the background was the main workshop of the original owners.

2000 More changes – a new forecourt for 'Jet'. Complete redesign provided an extensive range of household commodities, groceries, sweets, cigarettes, newspapers, magazines and alcoholic drinks. There was also a 'fast food' outlet with hot pies and snacks. The workshop was demolished and the area which was vacated provided space for apartments to be built in Elm Farm Avenue called Carter's Close.

2009 Even more change – new owners 'Murco Petroleum' and a new colour scheme.

Before the days of B&Q and other D.I.Y. Superstores there were a succession of private traders selling all manner of garden merchandise, tools, timber, corn, seeds, paint and pet foods. The first was 'Wyckham Blackwell' who traded at Station Road just short of Malthouse Row. It is not known how long they were there, but the 'Kelly's Trade Directory' of 1900 did not list them, but the 1938 version did have them listed as a 'corn and timber' merchant in Station Road. Unfortunately this is not correct. William Perkins followed Wyckham Blackwell and Frank Alcott was actually the trader at that address in 1938. In my earlier book, I noted that several Kelly Trade Directory listings were wildly inaccurate. I am sure that businessmen were keen to get their names included but rather slow to get them withdrawn.

1925. The hardware shop of William Perkins advertised his wares on the roof and walls of his premises. The lady on the right was a young Leah Griffin aged about 20, later she married Joe Martin and they lived at 'Holly Cottage' in Station Road.

Frank Allcott was the next trader carrying out the same activity as the previous owners. I believe that he was more successful than his predecessors, he appeared to have more stock which was more varied than before, especially garden tools which was certainly to meet the demands of the new homeholders emerging in the village at that time.

Frank Allcott, born in 1896, was an active personality and participated in many village activities. He served on the Parish Council for some 21 years and was Chairman of the Council for a number of years. During the war years, he was an Air Raid Warden (later Civil defence). Being on the Parish Council he was involved with the layout of the Memorial Garden.

Frank lived at 83, Station Road where he had a well equipped workshop at the bottom of his garden. He was a pattern maker by trade, but he was also a skilled engineer.

Frank Alcott was always producing machined items in his workshop, and as he was a good friend of my father, on occasions we were invited to his workshop to see the latest project that he would have been working on. He used to instruct local lads in the evenings on the basics of engineering and metal work.

Probably the most remarkable achievement that he will be remembered for is the 'Marston Green Model Engineering Club' which has been running for some 55 years and of which he was the original founder. His model steam train 'Speedy' ran at all of the village Festivals for years, both in Marston Green and at many other local shows around the district. The Club is still active after all these years.

1930 The following page shows the same shop with Frank Allcott in the doorway. The house next door was a private dwelling owned by Mrs. Maling and she rented out her

front room to 'Barclays Bank'. Bank literature indicated that they had moved there from Holly Lane in 1931, the opening hours were Tuesday and Thursday 11am to 12.15pm. The Bank closed during the war years. After the war from 1959 to 1962, the hours were Monday, Wednesday and Friday, 10am until 1.00pm. The new branch at 29, Station Road opened in 1962 with banking hours of Monday to Friday 10am. until 1.00pm. Present day the new opening hours are Monday to Friday 9.30am until 4.30pm.

1995 Some time later Frank Allcott moved to enlarged new premises in Elmdon Road. A series of Estate Agents took over and enlarged the premises to include the frontage vacated by Barclays Bank in 1962. The first occupier was 'Steeles', they were there for a number of years, followed by 'Contact Estates' then by 'Colin Johnson' who closed down in 2007. At the end of 2008, for the first time ever in Marston Green I believe, Funeral Directors took over the joint premises of Nos.48 and 50.

1990 The same premises again, but Nos.48 and 50 combined since the properties were opened up to accommodate the run of Estate Agents that continued up to 2007. The house on the left was built at the time when Frank Allcott was about to move to his new premises and took the place of the large storage building (seen on the previous page) of William Perkin's shop. I am not sure whether the flat above No.50 was ever in use again. Considering that we had three Estate Agents in the village for a considerable time, I wonder whether this particular location was a good place for that activity. No one seemed to last very long here, whilst the other two, being more central in the village always seemed to have more customers. Probably because people out shopping could walk and browse at the Agent's displayed properties, then get in their cars and drive past this location.

2008 'Franklin Funeral Directors' new occupants of Nos.48/50 Station Road.

'Franklin Family Funerals' are based in Tile Hill Lane, Coventry and have only been in business under their own name for some two years. Both the directors Gary Franklin and Andy Hawkins however, have spent many years in the funeral business and Gary spent many years employed by 'Painters' based at Yardley. Some years ago he was a resident of Marston Green. Their sales literature indicates that they are both committed to "providing the highest quality that goes beyond customers' expectations".

2009 The new store with enlarged warehouse that Frank Allcott built at No.4 Elmdon Road in the late 50s or early 60s, he traded there until his retirement. The premises have since been converted into an office complex and an earlier company were in the 'mail order business'.

At the present time there are four foreign companies sharing the building, the occupants are 'Pieroth Limited' – 'Vicomte Bernard De Romanet' – 'Nieredhaler Hof' and 'Pierrie La Forest'. My French is 5th form standard and German even worse, so I didn't attempt to enter the premises to find out what they did.

At the turn of the 19th Century there were no shops as we know them today, some cottagers did have notices at their premises advertising 'Teas and Cakes' and farmers would sell vegetables, fruit and dairy products. But retailers were not known.

Changes did come however, in 1910 a few shops around the Station area opened up. A private grocer named 'Croad' was one of the first and alongside came a newsagents called the 'Kiosk', and in Holly Lane Mrs. Louisa Bates, a pharmacist opened the 'Chelmsley Drug Store'.

In the mid 20s in Station Road, opposite what was 'Malt House Farm' three pairs of self contained shops opened, and are still there today, albeit with different retail outlets to what they began as some 80 years ago. The main selection of new shops were centred in Station Road opposite the 'Tavern' but they didn't all arrive at the same time. The row extending from what (until recently) was the Estate Agents to the Fish and Chip Shop, came in 1938/39. The war prevented any more building and the final new shops from 'Barretts' up to 'Barclays Bank' did not arrive until the late 50s, early 60s.

The three pairs of semi-detached shops further down Station Road number from No.58, nearest to Malthouse Row up to No.68. The present day shop 'Handful of Flowers' was for most of its 80 years existence a General Store and Sweet Shop owned by the 'Osborne' family.

Frank Osborne the owner was there at first with his daughter Jessie, then on his retirement handed over to his son, Sam, and his wife. In their shop was a prominent notice which was blunt, but to the point "We don't ask for credit – and we don't give it". To the left of the property extending towards Malthouse Row was a lawned area laid out with tables and chairs in the summer for 'Afternoon Teas' which was very popular in summer months – we did have warm summers in those days.

They retired in the late 1980s, there were then two planning applications – an Indian Curry House and a Solicitors Office, both turned down because of "change of use from retail outlet".

2009 'Handful of Flowers' – colourful display on Mother's Day.

Finally, Sharon Parfrey arrived in 1991 as the owner of 'Handful of Flowers' and has been very successful, her staff are very friendly and obliging and nowadays there is a full time van delivery service around the district.

Next door at No.60 is the village Pharmacy, Ronald Campbell was the first Chemist in 1925 and he was there until 1945. Quite amazingly there have only been four others since then.

1995 The 'Pharmacy' No.60 Station Road.

Prior to this Pharmacy being opened there was an earlier Drug Store at No.7 Holly Lane, which was multi-functional as the owner Mrs. Louisa Bates carried out other activities at the premises. The first 'true' Pharmacy was at this location with Ronald Campbell as the Pharmaceutical Chemist, he was there from 1925 until 1945. He was followed with approximate dates by:

Robert Broughton 1945 until 1970
Robert Magson 1970 until 2000
Punian 2000 until 2007
Adam Myers 2007 (still counting)

Whilst many other shops in the village have changed hands or retail outlets, No.60 is not only still a chemist, but amazingly, until September 2009, the premises had not changed structurally since it was first built in 1925.

No.62 Station Road has, for most of its time, been a greengrocer's, the first was Sydney Corbett and he was there for some years before the war, but there may have been a J.T.Chance just prior to the war. Immediately after the war Stan Starkey was the occupier and he was there during the 1950s and into the late 1960s. He was followed by 'Mar-Jon' who advertised themselves as 'Fruit/Greengrocery/Flowers and Fresh Fish daily'. Several greengrocers followed, none of them staying very long, the Hileys, the Wards and Smiths who were the last. There was then a change of usage as George Taplin having retired from the teaching profession opened a book shop from 1990 until 2002.

Another change came at George's retirement as a Ladies Hairdressing Salon called 'Studio 64' opened up there which does seem rather confusing as to the apparent anomaly as to why 'Studio 64' at No.62.

The hairdressing salon was opened by the 'Pretty' girls, Sarah and Maria who previously had worked for some 12 years at Stephen Henri's Ladies' Hairdressers Shop, (now called 'Heavan Sent'). They decided to open up on their own, and moved to No.64 Station Road (hence the name 'Studio 64') in 1999, but after just 4 years they moved next door to No.62 but kept their original name.

In 1925 when No.64 first opened, the first tradesman was Alfred Edward Thomas a Plumber and Gasfitter, and in those early days his Sales Literature indicated that "Forms were available for ordering Meters, Stoves, Gas Fires on Application". He also pointed out that his shop was "Closed on Wednesdays" and in fact it was the general practice as a 'half day' closing for Shopkeepers in those days. My father regularly played football in the winter, and cricket in the summer in various local 'Wednesday early closing' leagues. Mr. Thomas was wounded in the first world war and rode his tradesman's cycle around the village using just one pedal as he was unable to bend his other leg due to the injury to his knee. He remained in business until 1951.

Following Mr. Thomas was a firm called 'Yardley Radio Stores' and their brochures stated that they were Agents for 'Bush', 'Phillips', 'H.M.V.', 'Pye', 'Connor' and 'Ferguson' – these were early days for television, a popular model was '9 inch'. They were there from 1951 until 1954 when they moved to 43, Station Road.

In 1955 a 'local lad' named Rex Hanson moved into the premises as an Electrical Engineer and Contractor having earlier operated from his home address in Elmdon Lane. Rex employed another local named Alec Weaver, the son of the Marston Green Station Master William George Weaver.

In the shop Rex offered a complete range of electrical goods, household fitments, aerials, televisions, wirelesses, vacuum cleaners.etc. As a testament as to how much Rex appreciated Alec's contribution to the success of the business, he delayed his own retirement until Alec reached his in 1980.

After Rex, a Roy Wilson opened a Picture Framing Business at No.64 for a short while, probably less than 4 years and it then remained empty until Sharon Parfrey from 'Handful of Flowers' opened a 'Party Shop' in 2007 which catered for mainly children's parties, with qualified balloon decorators, animal features etc. but she closed the outlet after some 18 months, and at the moment it is empty once again.

When No.66 opened it was an agency trading under the name of 'Wimbushes' who at that time were a leading bread and cake manufacturer. The owner was Mr. H.Clark a local man who lived across the road at No.83 Station Road. He remained at the premises until 1950 and presumably ill health forced his retirement as at that time after his wife died, there was considerable concern as to his state of mind as it became known that he kept a horse in his dining room.

For many years after Mr. Clark there were a series of owners who continued with the same business as agent's for 'Wimbushes' but increased their outlets to include groceries and provisions. The first were 'Grewcocks' who were there from 1951 until 1963, followed by W.E. and N.Egan, 1963 until 1969, then Jutland J.Oakley and finally the last ones carrying out as retail grocery suppliers were Jim and June Gibney.

In 1994 a firm called 'Care Home' took over and provided equipment and services for the disabled. They remained until 2006 and then moved to premises in Sheldon and presumably a larger catchment area for disabled and less mobile customers.

No.66 then changed its function again and became a Gent's 'Barbers Shop' and advertising the option of 'Hair Art' by Mitch, having previously operated from 57a, adjacent to 'Heavan Sent' for some three years.

2009 Nos.66 and 68 Station Road.

143

The last premises in the row of shops was a Ladies' and Childrens' Outfitters with a Miss Hutchison as the first owner, she was there until the late 1940s when Mrs. Macey took over. She also remained for many years until the mid 1990s when a creche then opened called 'Wellies' which catered for youngsters below the age for admittance at the Marston Green Infants School.

1950 The photograph above shows the first of the shops built in 1938/39, which were located opposite the 'Tavern' numbered 37 to 51 Station Road. They were built with pseudo-oak facade which gave them a 'wordly' appearance in line with the old cottages that were around the village at that time. The road past the end shop was Elm Farm Avenue, opened at the same time. The large building beyond was the Telephone Exchange, and outside the shops was the service road, obviously catering for cycles in those days. The lady standing by the fence is waiting for the 'Midland Red' to Birmingham terminating at St. Martin's Church in those days.

Behind the fence was an open field which extended to the back of the houses in Elm Farm Avenue and up to what was 'Wrenson's Grocery Store' at that time.

The first occupants of No.37, which was the Fish and Chip Shop, were the 'Ludlows'. They had a son Ralf and they stayed through the war years until 1945 when they emigrated to Australia. They were followed by 'Shelton and Green', (seen on the photo') for a few years then by 'Grinnells', both of them added fruit and vegetables to their sales options. Toni Georgiou, the present occupier was told that Mrs. Grinnell and her sister came from Blackpool. That may well be true, but earlier Mrs. Grinnell and her family came from Oldknow Road in Small Heath, her daughter Pat married a local lad Barry Thompson, who lived in the family home of butcher Les Thompson in Elmdon Road opposite the Village Hall, along with a younger brother Roy who continued in the butchery business at Green Lane, Small Heath for many years.

TRADESMEN AND SHOPKEEPER'S – 1950

After the 'Grinnells' a gentleman by the name of 'Tomlin' was there for a few years, then 'Andy and Thelga' and finally after these changes some continuity arrived when a Greek Cypriot family came along in 1994 with Tony Georgiou and he has maintained the long chain of 'chippies' in the village.

The shop next door, No.39 has been a Ladies' Hairdressers from the start. An early starter was a Mrs. Ponting trading under the name of 'Vallenna' and she continued until 'Tony' arrived in 1979. Since then his business has been consistent and well patronised and has remained, which cannot be said for most of his competitors.

2009 Nos.37 to 41 Station Road.

No.41 has had numerous outlets over the years. In 1938 a Ladies' and Children's Outfitters were there trading under the name of 'Kays' with a Mrs. B.I.Holder as the proprietor, she was still operating up to 1950. In 1951 a shop called 'Bones' took over adding 'baby wear, wools and hosiery' to their sales. They were followed by 'Powells' and later still by Mrs. Morgan. A change of usage came then in 1996 when 'Impress Dry Cleaners' operating a laundry service took over the premises and are still operating a much appreciated service.

A local man Joe Knight, an Electrical Contractor was the first tradesman at No.43. He unfortunately, did not last long as he had an untimely death whilst carrying out an electrical installation. He was followed by 'Yardley Radio and Television' who had earlier been at No.64 Station Road. For a short while in the 1960s, J.M.Yates was there selling 'General Drapery, Dry Cleaning and Materials'. Then another change when 'Regency Bookmakers' moved in. Present occupiers are 'William Hill' another Bookmaker and they have been there ever since the gambling laws were changed back in the early 1960s.

2009 Nos.43 and 45 Station Road.

No.45 was not occupied during the war years, although the flat above was in use. The Hardman family lived there having moved from Stoke on Trent. The Hardmans had 4 daughters, Margaret (later wife of George Cuthbertson), Dorothy, Gwen and Barbara.

After the war Mrs. French had a Wallpaper, Hardware and Ironmongery Shop there. She was followed by 'Mitchells' operating in the same retail business. Later the shop became a 'Laundrette' for some 20 years, and recently in the last couple of years the premises have been taken over by 'Subway' a hot food and sandwich outlet.

2009 Nos.47 and 49 Station Road.

In the early days No.47 continued for many years as a 'Tobacconist, Confectioners and Stationery' outlet. They however had many changes of ownership, 'Rothmans' were the original occupants and they also ran a 'lending library'. They were followed by 'Bartons' then 'Fields' who were there for a long time. 'G.J. and E.Turner' were there in the 1960s. 'Roland Quiney' was there for a few years and finally with the same retail outlet was a shop just called 'Devs'. It then remained closed for some time and in the mid 1990s a new business arrived called 'So Naturelle' who advertised themselves as a 'Health and Beauty Retreat'.

No.49 was originally 'Baines and Head' who sold bread, cakes, cooked meats, etc. During war time there was a character in the village called 'Tom Shanty' who was, to say the least, awkward. He was very religious, he was anti-war and he refused to accept Identity Cards and Ration Books for food which were issued to everyone. The two ladies at 'Baines and Head' at the end of each week used to give him bread, and cooked meats to help him. After the ladies retired, Mr. Barton from next door took over for a while. After that the 'Reardon' family took over, and in the 1950s 'Jayne's Pantry' came and remained for a number of years. The recent owners are advertised as the 'Marston Green Chop Suey House' and they have been there since 1997.

The last property in the row of shops is No.51 and was originally opened as a 'Clock and Watch Repairer' with Mr. W.H.Edwards as the proprietor. He was followed fairly quickly by a 'bespoke tailor' named Tulk who had moved from the wooden store which formally belonged to 'Griffins' when they sold cycles. In the 1950s the 'Midland Bank' (later H.S.B.C.) opened as a subsidiary of the Coleshill branch, but eventually closed in the 1980s. The Estate Agents 'Burchell Edwards' came next and remained until they were hit by the recession and closed in 2008. It is still 'shuttered' and has been closed ever since.

2005 'Burchell Edwards' whilst still an active trading Estate Agents were probably for some time, the first choice amongst those looking for, or hoping to sell at that time.

However, as trading got difficult and as the premises were only a 'branch office' when it closed, Marston Green houses are now covered by the main office in High Street, Solihull.

As mentioned earlier after the war there was only a field from the Fish and Chip Shop at No.37 up to 'Wrenson's' the Grocers (later Flair), and at a point just a few yards from the Fish and Chip was an uncovered 'Midland Red' bus stop.

However, at the same place there was a much publicised notice which had been there since pre-war days indicating that Marston Green would at some time have a 'New Super Cinema' called the 'Clifton'. The notice was displayed and placed in the field hedge just to the right of the Fish and Chip Shop.

Apparently, after the war had ended, it was noticed that the hedge along the boundary of the field was overgrown and was in need of urgent pruning, and as a result, the notice which had been hidden and forgotten, became visible again.

The Parish Council made extensive enquiries via the Architect whose name was on the board. He contacted the Estate Agent who was sorry, but he was unable to find out who the field belonged to.

So sadly, because communications and correspondence between people whose names were prominently displayed and unknown persons who would or should have been involved, having apparently gone astray, and the small matter of the Second World War intervening, we never had our eagerly expected Cinema.

However, despite the doubts expressed as to who were the owners of the field, surprise, surprise, not too much later in the late 1950s or early 1960s, 3 pairs of semi-detached houses and 4 double fronted shops were soon erected in the same field. The houses were numbered Nos.17 to 27, and the Shops Nos.29 to 35.

Simultaneously, a new road appeared at the far end of the field called 'Marston Croft' and even more houses.

Perhaps the reason that we lost our cinema was that the aforementioned houses and shops were financially a better option than a Cinema – we shall never know!

The first occupants of the individual shops were 'Greens' sports outfitters, trading under the name of 'Olympic House' at No.29, and 'Boots the Chemists' were at No.31, then came a Ladies' Hairdressers called 'Vanity Faire' at No.33 and finally a shop called 'Variety Stores' owned by a man called George who sold fruit, vegetables, bedding plants, compost and growbags and Christmas trees in December.

Green's the sports outfitters at No.29 originated from their business on the Coventry Road in Small Heath and was quite an impressive shop. They had an extensive range of Slazenger's tennis equipment, Dunlop football, and golf clubs and Wisden cricket bats and associated gear. They also sold toys and games, peerage brass ware, Tri-ang and Dinky toys, Smith's clocks, Parker pens, etc. Despite all this they never quite took off in Marston Green and they closed in the late 1950s.

They were followed by Barclays Bank who opened in 1962 having previously operated from No.7 Holly Lane and No.50 Station Road for many years apart from the war years when they closed the branch in Station Road.

No.31 was another well known company – Boots the Chemists. The village already had an established and popular chemist in Ron Campbell and 'Boots' only lasted for a few years and then closed. A local villager John Piff followed and opened a D.I.Y. Shop before the days of

1989 Nos.29 and 31 Station Road.

B&Q and Homebase. John was in business for some 15 to 20 years but closed in the 1980s.

They were followed by a retailer selling mainly groceries called 'The Village Stores' and were well supported and were in business for probably 20 years. More recently Mills the newsagents who were close to the Station, bought up the premises opening a second shop in the mid 2000s, continuing in the same line but offering a greater line in groceries, frozen foods and more significantly with a drinks licence.

2009 Nos.29 and 31 Station Road.

The third shop that opened was a Ladies' Hairdressers called 'Vanity Faire'. Originally it was a double fronted shop like the other shops in the row, but at some point they reduced the width of the shop and created No.33a. Part of the shop nearest to Barretts was a narrow shop which opened as a 'barbers shop' with 'Joe' as the proprietor, we never knew his surname, he always said "Just call me Joe". Above the shop a 'Taxi firm' operated a direct telephone call service for a few years.

'Hazey Fantazey' also a Ladies' Hairdressers followed 'Vanity Faire' in 1984, and at that time the 'barber's shop' had disappeared as had the 'Taxi' business. A video hire firm had arrived called 'Premier Video Club' which took over No.33a. They were there up to the early 2000s and some 8 years ago a greetings card shop arrived called 'Wishes Card and Gift Shop'.

The last shop in the row No.35 was called 'Variety Store' and the owner George Knight certainly managed to relate to the name of the store. Primarily he was a greengrocer selling fruit and vegetables, but he also sold bedding plants, compost, grow bags and all manner of garden accessories, and late in the year he stocked a wide range of Christmas trees of all shapes and sizes. He ceased trading in the late 1980s and the store remained empty for two or three years.

Then Mike Barrett took over and opened his butchery business having previously been in business at No.9 Land Lane for about three years. Mike used both sides of the shop and apart from the butchery business, he provided a 'takeaway' service of hot

and cold sandwiches and rolls, cooked meats, bread and cakes. It is very popular early morning and there is always a steady stream of customers.

1948 Looking towards the village shops in Station Road, the dual carriageway was created immediately prior to the war in 1937/38. Beyond the shops on the right can be seen the Telephone Exchange. The fenced field on the left belongs to 'Mitchells and Butlers' and the notice indicates that the land is for sale. The building beyond was 'Whitehead's Cottage' and the tall chimneys belonged to the old 'Tavern'.

TRADESMEN AND SHOPKEEPER'S-2009

On the earlier 1930 photograph taken from the same viewpoint can be seen the beautiful chestnut tree which, along with several more mature trees, was removed to allow for the introduction of the 'barren' appearance dual carriage way. The solitary tree at the front was planted to take the place of the one that was felled. It will probably take some 200 years to reach the same size.

Shortly after the photograph was taken, the new houses extending from the shops towards Holly Lane would have been started and the 'cul de sac' Marston Croft to the left of 'Wrensons' at about the same time. Cycles were still evident as a useful form of transport around the village, I bought my first car about that time – a 1928 Austin 7, which did some 55 miles per hour, down hill, with a wind behind.

As mentioned earlier my father came to Marston Green in 1928 and replaced Mr. Cochrane as Manager of the 'Wrensons Store' in Station Road. Later in 1930 he moved across the road into Holly Lane and bought the premises known as 'The Chelmsley Drug Store' which had, up to 5 years previously been the village Pharmacy.

The premises at that time comprised 4 bedroomed accommodation with a kitchen behind the grocery section of the shop and a lounge behind the greengrocery area.

The smaller shop on the left was a 'Hairdressing Salon' owned by Marion Blamire and as a result of my father taking over the whole premises, the Salon moved next door to No11. Holly Lane. Marion Blamire had a sister who operated from the same address and she was very popular as she ran a 'home visit Chiropody' service around the village. The Blamires lived at a windmill at Berkswell, which quite coincidentally has recently been restored.

The driveway between the two properties belonged to a firm called 'H.R. Thermostats' and their workshop was located at the rear of the Holly Lane houses.

For some time, the kitchen was used as a 'temporary office' and the lounge area became the store where the provisions were prepared for display in the shop. For some months we moved to a semi-detached house in Elmdon Lane between Land Lane and Elmdon Road whilst modifications were made to the shop and new living accommodation added above the shop premises.

1930 The original 'Crawford's Stores' in Holly Lane shortly after opening as a Grocery and Greengrocery Store.

In the photo my father Edmund Crawford is the central person, with Len Priddey on the left and Tom Higgs on the right. I do not recall who the two ladies outside the Greengrocery shop were but there was also another lady who looked after the bookkeeping.

Before the days of Supermarkets, Crawford's Stores were the largest privately owned Grocery and Greengrocery Shop in Warwickshire. At one time the staff numbered 12, and deliveries were made to individual households each week by errand boys using carrier bikes in the village. Each customer had an order book which was handed in at the shop or collected by members of staff. Van deliveries were made to other villages, Bickenhill, Elmdon, Meriden, Hampton in Arden, Berkswell and one customer, a farmer named Green lived as far away as Atherstone and had a monthly order delivered.

1940 Predominantly male staff in the early days of the war. Left to right are Gordon Buckley, Alf Rawlins, George Burgess, Bill Harrow, Les Buckley, 'Pop' Etherington, Ray Crook, Sheila Agnew, Elsie Dewick, Sidney Heath-Woodward and Reg Statham. Most of those pictured were called up for military Service later that year.

1943 The ladies of the 'war time staff'. On the left Kitty Gallahar (later Harrow), Doris Wilkinson (later Rose), Josephine Holdnall, Sheila Hall and Elsie Bennett. On the right in the doorway Vera Colloby and Dorothy Weaver (later Wilson). All the plums and apples were picked by the Crawford family at a relative's farm called 'Primsland Farm' at Hadzor (Archer's country) near Droitwich in Worcestershire, the day before. Fruit did not require 'ration book' coupons.

This farm house being way off the main road was more or less cut off for some time by deep snow and horrendous storms in January 1940, I believe. I and many other lads from the village used to walk to school at Coleshill for quite a long time, with snow several inches deep and snowdrifts which prevented local bus services operating.

At the store, an old gentleman named 'Pop' Etherington was fully occupied in wrapping grocery produce into suitable weights, as most commodities were delivered in bulk, such as loose tea, butter, sugar, cheese, raisins, currants, sultanas, etc. After the war my father sold out to the 'Birmingham Co-operative Society' and for many years the business traded simply as a Grocery Store. The number of customers declined over a period of time, caused it was thought by the fact that villagers did not like the D.I.Y. style of shopping introduced by the Co-op.

Eventually, the premises became an outdoor, selling wines, spirits, beers and soft drinks. Then in the late 1990s they renamed themselves 'The Village Store' and once again a range of household goods and other commodities became available whilst continuing with wines, beer and spirits. A few years ago they changed their name once more and trade simply as Drinks Stop.

On the other side of Holly Lane there were several shops and tradesmen. The properties were built in the period 1925/26 and were numbered from No.8 up to

2009 The 'Drinks Stop' shop in Holly Lane.

No.38 which stood some 20 yards short of Moseley Drive. No.8 was the home of Mr. Jenkins the local Chimney Sweep, further along at No.20 was a butcher's Shop managed by Alf Thompson, one of the sons of Charles Thompson, founder of the family butchery business. Alfred was there for over 30 years. Since he retired in the 1960s there have been other butchers at the same address, Ray Bill was the first, followed by Peter Jacobs (later of 'Flair'), then a Mr. Freeman and finally at the time of closure, Steve Eaton and family. At some time in the late 1980s, early 1990s the frontage and the shop interior were removed and the building reverted to a family residence with Peter Jacobs, now retired, living there.

The pair of semi-detached houses Nos.22 and 24 next door were built just before the war and were occupied by the 'Bates' and 'Wallace' families. The Bates had a daughter Margaret and she married a long time resident of the village Eric Brelsford and they lived at a bungalow in Coleshill Heath Road. William Bates was manager of the Staff Salaries Department at Metropolitan Cammell Company at Saltley. The 'Wallaces' had a son Brian and they emigrated to Australia at the end of the war.

2009 No. 26 restored to a private residence.

At the rear of their properties were several large greenhouses where Archie Bachelor operated as a Nurseryman. Archie and his wife lived at No.26 where his wife ran a sweet shop. When he retired the father of Molly Jones took over the Nursery. The Jones at that time lived at No.18 but later Molly and her husband moved to No.23 on the other side of Holly Lane. Again No.26 which was for some 30 years a sweet shop, was converted back to a private residence probably in the 1960s and until quite recently Stella Reece's mother lived there. The Greenhouses have long since disappeared but between No.24 and No.26 there is close boarded fencing still to be seen which used to be the gateway to the Nursery.

Further along Holly Lane is No.28 which is where the 'Riley' Family lived. Vic Riley was a very lucky man during the war as his house was hit by the last bomb of a stick of bombs which crossed Elmdon Lane and past the Station. He had left the Anderson Shelter at the bottom of his garden to make a pot of tea, on the way back to the shelter, the bomb fell and demolished part of the house. The house was rebuilt and apparently when it was completed, the house was larger than the undamaged half of the semi-detached next door at No.30.

Further down were two semi-detached shops No.s 32 and 32a. My first memory of No.32 the left hand shop was as 'Insall's Gents Hairdressers' with a Mr. Barraclough as Manager, he was pre-war days and retired in the '50s. After that came a Greengrocers belonging to the Co-op, with Tom Shields as the Manager which closed after a few years. It was then taken over by Ray Smith and his wife with an Electrical Contracting business and they remained for close to 40 years. It then stood empty for a few years and recently about 2007/08 a company called 'the freight shop' arrived advertising that they specialise in "Parcels, Baggage and Freight to the world".

No.32a started as a Co-op Butcher's Shop with Mr. Morrell as Manager and he had a young assistant Peter Jacobs. The next occupants in 1964 caused quite a stir in the village when a notice in their window indicated that a Bookmaker intended to open a 'Betting Shop'. Letters of complaint supported by the Parish Council were sent to the Licensing Authorities, all to no avail as the approval had already been passed.

Further events followed, Mr. Brown was the first Bookmaker, and he didn't stop long and when he left the 'proceeds' went with him. 'Cutlers' a reputable Bookmaker then took over and some years later 'Coral' arrived. Sadly, the Manager was hit on the head and the assailants got away with the takings. Later an investigation revealed that the robbery was an inside job. The bookies left and a less hazardous occupation came when 'Maginnis' the Opticians took over who are still with us.

Across the road No.11, which originally was a private dwelling, but in 1930 became a Ladies Hairdressers with Marion Blamire as joint owner with her Chiropodist sister, eventually closed down in the late 1950s. For some time the Chiropodist Blamire, continued working well past her 70th birthday from a rented room at No.8 belonging to Mr. Jenkins the local Chimney Sweep. After closure as a Hairdressers the shop continued in business, first of all as a Dress Shop for about 12 years, it then became a Flower Shop, and for a few years until it finally closed down in the mid 1990s, it sold Gent's Shirts and Ties. Then like the two properties Nos.20 and 26, it reverted to its original use as a private dwelling.

2009 No.11 Holly Lane restored back to a private residence.

2009 No.3 Station Road, continuing as the longest serving village shop operating for almost 100 years in the same business as a Newsagent.

The newsagent's, considering how many years it has operated, is surprising as there have only been probably five changes in ownership. I know that Mr. Atack was there in the early 1930s as I went to school with Stan Atack his son and I believe that he was the original owner when it opened. He was followed by Mr. Smith in 1935 as an early photograph indicated newspaper 'billboards' with the headlines "Britain to make Arms Statement" and "Roosevelt's Dramatic Appeal". Mr. Smith remained until the 1960s and was replaced by Norman James who was there until the early 1990s when a newsagency firm named 'Morgam News' arrived who more recently were taken over by 'Mills' the present occupiers in the early 2000s.

2009 Flair Door Centre showing their new show room.

As mentioned earlier the premises were originally a private grocery store owned by a man named 'Croad', he sold out to a large Birmingham Grocery Company called 'Wrensons' in about 1920. They remained until closure in 1970, almost certainly because of the arrival of supermarkets, and in that period they had three Managers, Mr. Cochrane (1920 to 1928), my father Edmund Crawford (1928 to 1930) and Harry Haines (1970 until closure).

'Flair' was originally a D.I.Y. Store operating from the old grocery premises, selling timber, paints, fencing panels, glass panels, garden accessories, growbags, fertilisers , bedding plants, etc. Peter Jacobs was the owner and it became a family business as several of his immediate family have worked there over the years.

In 2005 there was a change in retail sales when they enlarged the premises by adding a new show room which predominately specialised in doors and associated fitments. Peter Jacobs remains as the owner but has recently opted for a semi-retirement role.

For most of its existence No.6 Holly Lane operated purely as a confectionary shop selling sweets, cakes, bread and cigarettes managed by Hetty Holder. I believe that she retired in the 1980s. Since then it has traded under the name of 'The Picnic Basket' which was owned by two gentlemen who prepared, sold and delivered sandwiches to a number of business premises around the village. They were there for a few years and later were taken over by a married couple up to 2000.

The present owner is Rachel Dowling who continues with the same activities, offering hot and cold sandwiches, baguettes, hot dogs and hamburgers and she appears to have regular external clients, as her van is frequently seen most weekdays operating the delivery service. Subject to weather conditions, customers can enjoy early morning breakfast sitting outside on the shop frontage.

2009 The Picnic Basket in Holly Lane.

2009 Looking down the village with replacement chestnut tree.

On the Land Lane corner next door to the Post Office is a building which is at present called 'The Tea Room' and also caters as a Chinese Restaurant and which has stood there for over 70 years. In the mid 1920s it was called 'Wilson's Suburban Stores' and was a popular spot during spring and summer months as it was on the direct route from Marston Green Station through to Chelmsley Woods. In April and early May the bluebells used to be a major attraction and train load after train load used to drop off large numbers of parents with their children who made a 'pilgrimage' to pick the bluebells. Wilson's Store was in an ideal location for weary 'moms and dads' to stop for afternoon 'tea and cakes' whilst the children enjoyed ice creams and glasses of lemonade. The Stores were kept by the grandmother of Ron Wilson.

After the 'Wilsons' came the 'Jones' and whilst their intentions were to carry on as before, but they turned themselves into more of a general store and probably had more customers buying groceries and the odd cup of tea, the restaurant trade diminished.

Later of course, houses were built on the tea gardens round the corner into Allcott Lane which put an end to the tea gardens.

1938 'Wilson's Tea Rooms' and Gardens in Allcott Lane.

1938 No.3 Allcott Lane 'Wilson's Suburban Store' The boards advertise Cream Ices and 'Whites' Lemonade, not clear what commodities are on display but a selection of potted plants and small shrubs were often sold. After the 'Jones' an Italian Restaurant called 'Baccos' arrived, they carried out structural changes to the premises, adding extra rooms to the first floor and a new roof.

2009 'Baccos' had a good reputation and had a varied selections of meals on offer as well as traditional Italian menus. But a change of cuisine came in mid 2000s from Italian to Chinese and they too have carried out minor structural improvements and refurbishment and now call themselves 'The Tea Room'.

Chapter 22

FORMER SHOPKEEPERS

IN LAND Lane there were five separate shops which over the years had changes, both to occupiers and also to the retail outlets.

The two houses at the far end were both shops for many years, No.5 was a Grocery Shop owned by Mr. H.C. Smith, he had been there pre-war and for a number of years after. He was followed by Mrs.

1999 Nos.5 and No.7 Land Lane.

Pat Bone, she remained there for a few years but after she ceased trading, there were two other owners who carried on for a short while but it was finally turned into a private residence.

A similar story related to No.7 next door, the shop was a green grocers for many years prior to pre war days with 'Blizzards' as the proprietors, but later in the early 1960s 'Dot' Simpson and her husband took over. Dot looked after the shop and her husband ran a mobile 'door to door' delivery service. When they ceased trading in 1989 the property was also converted to a private residence. The Simpsons moved to a new house in Chelmsley Lane but when Dot's husband passed away some 4 years later she moved back into her former business premises with one of her sons, and has recently reached the anniversary of 50 years since coming to Marston Green.

No.9 shown as a Motor Cycle Spares Shop started out as a General Store owned by Mrs. Dora Sharp. But in 1925 she extended her business and took over as village Post Mistress, due to the closure of the earlier Post Office which had also been situated in Land Lane at No.2 'The Cottage' opposite the present Clinic.

She must have been pleased at her new status as she had two prominent Post Office notices advertising the fact at the front of the premises. But her tenure was short lived as in 1929 Frank Aston opened his family butchery business there, which

1925 No.9 Land Lane Mrs. Dora Sharp – Post Mistress.

1950 The Aston's Shop in Land Lane for many years was a thriving family business but the arrival of 'supermarkets' had much to do with them prematurely closing in the late 1980s. The shop remained closed for a few years but eventually Mike Barrett re-opened the premises also as a butcher. He stayed there for two or three years and then moved to a larger shop at No.35 in Station Road.

1990 Mike Barrett when his Butcher's Shop was in Land Lane.

was the start of some 70 years of butchery at the premises.

The earlier Post Office with Mr. Jeffs as Sub Post Master closed because shoe repairer Albert Knibbs bought No.2 Land Lane in 1925 and moved in.

Frank Aston the first of the Aston family ran the butchery business from No.9 in Land Lane, followed by his son Reginald shortly after the war finished and then finally by grandson George. In 1951 when Marston Green took part in the 'Festival of Britain Week', Reg Aston displayed an advert in the celebratory programme "Get your share of unrationed goods" indicating that although the war had been over some 6 years the country still had some restrictions on what foods were still freely available. George Aston was an active Parish Councillor for many years including a number of years as Chairman.

The present occupants of No.9 are 'C. and C. Motor Cycle Products' believed to be a Cox family. They have been in business for a number of years and used to operate from the small businesses that were based at the old barns that remained after 'Hall Farm' was demolished in Elmdon Road. They had a 'french polishing business' whilst they were there at that time. At the moment their speciality is provision of Motor Cycle Exhausts.

Nos.11 an 13, the last two shops were 'Jones and Walford'

who were Drapers. They were followed by Mrs. Broadhead. Next door was an Electrical and Television Shop owned by Cyril Driscoll, he remained in business until the 1960s and retired to his bungalow in Chelmsley Lane where he recently passed away in his 93rd year.

Both premises were then taken over by a firm of Exhibition Organisers for some time as seen on the 1999 photograph, but at the moment 'Family Care Trust' – Solihull have the premises.

At the rear of the building many years ago there was a builder's yard belonging to George Foster who was prominent in building many houses in Elmdon Lane both before and after the war. Later, Hire Tools were available from a Mr. T. Price. Despite extensive extensions at the rear there does not appear to be any activity happening at the present time.

Based on the cross roads of Land Lane and Elmdon Road there have been a number of businesses operating from time to time but present day, only 'Ye Olde Village Wine Lodge' actually started out in the same line of business.

1928 Properties around the Elmdon Road/Land Lane junction.

No.8 Land Lane, the shop on the immediate left was a grocery shop belonging to the 'Mowe' family with Harriett, wife of John Mowe running the shop. John Mowe was a signalman and came from Bulkington, his wife from London. However in the 1901 Census they were in Marston Green, John aged 37 and Harriett 35, with their 6 daughters. I believe that the Mowes were around in the village well after 1901 as when I wrote my first book some older residents remembered him.

The shop continued for many years with the same retail outlet of grocery, firstly with 'Masons' who were there into the 1960s, and they were followed by 'Bishops' who I believe were the last traders from the premises.

Beyond at No.9 was John Lloyd who had a butchery business. John farmed in Bickenhill and he took over the Butcher's Shop after the earlier butcher, Frank Abbott was killed when he was knocked off his bike in Coleshill. At the rear of his shop there was an abattoir where John brought his own cattle for slaughter. John was in business before the war and he continued until the shop finally closed down.

The other two buildings on the left were No.7 'Alden' which was the family home of 'Bill' Knibbs, the village Post Man. According to daughter Hilda Elliott, (wife of Charles) the house was built in 1927 and the other two buildings were built earlier, probably in 1925 when most of the houses were built at that time.

After the grocery shop ceased trading the premises were taken over by Solicitors, firstly by 'Bond Lassen' with Audrey Bond and Caroline Lassen being the partners, and

1999 The Solicitors 'Wallace, Robinson and Morgan'.

later by a firm of Solicitors called 'Wallace, Robinson and Morgan'. In that period of time the butchers shop was demolished and modern flats called 'Elmdon Court' were built at the same location.

They were in business for some 25 years but were not to survive the recession and closed down in 2008. The premises were empty for 2 years but recently have been taken over as offices for the Management Staff of the Family Care Trust (Solihull) which is a Registered Charity and who were previously situated at their other premises across the road in Land Lane.

Behind on the left is the complex known as 'Elmdon Court' which comprises 8 two bedroomed apartments and 2 semi-detached ground floor flats.

2009 'Elmdon Court' in Elmdon Road.

Just outside the actual confines of the village, opposite to the newly named 'Bell' inn there used to be a blacksmith's forge who operated there probably for some 200 years in pre war days until closure in the 1950s. There were two old cottages alongside the Smithy, and prior to the arrival of the railway the area behind the buildings was open land extending to Sheldon known as 'Radley Moor'.

1910 The Blacksmith's Forge in Bell Lane. An early Blacksmith was John Wheeler, but at the time of the closure, Fred Stanton was the man who carried on the business and looked after the declining needs of the local farming community.

1930 Fred Stanton, the Blacksmith and his mate outside the forge in Bell Lane when it was a thriving business.

Across the road, pre war and for a short while afterwards there used to be a business who manufactured a variety of sweets owned by Charles Moseley and his brothers, Reg and Ted. Nowadays there is a secure lock up storage company at the premises.

At the Black Firs end of the village, there were prior to the last war quite a number of cottages and houses, the cottages being primarily in Black Firs Lane, which in those days did continue out to the Chester Road (A452). Most of the houses were on Bickenhill Lane which nowadays are in the section which has been 'by-passed'.

Amongst those houses was one which traded as a shop offering sweets, confectionery and other commodities. The house was called 'Newman' which belonged to Mrs. Anne Harvey, and because of the distance from the village it was very popular and well frequented (not many people had cars in those days) by her immediate neighbours. She remained in business for a short time after the war had ended.

1950 House 'Newman' in Bickenhill Lane.

At the junction of Coleshill Heath Road with the Chester Road which has been identified on old maps always as 'Windy Arbour' there were two quite old cottages on the left hand side, opposite where a number of present day buses use as their termini.

One of the cottages did sell sweets and confectionery. They were still there during the war years but were demolished soon after.

Chapter 23

POST WAR HOUSING

THE FIRST building in the village after the end of the war comprised 28 council houses which were built some 50 yards short of the bridge crossing Low Brook on the right hand side, off Bickenhill Road. The houses were Swedish sectional design, basically made from timber, and they had the advantage of being easily erected with the individual sections simply bolting together. The properties were semi-detached units, 6 bungalows were added later and the new housing was called 'Lyndon Croft'.

2009 'Lyndon Croft' was built as a 'cul de sac' with properties on both sides of the roadway extending up to the facing houses in the photograph, seen beyond the grassed circular island.

Lyndon Croft were in fact the second council houses built in the village as earlier in 1928, 6 houses were built on the corner of Bickenhill Lane and Black Firs Lane.

The next houses built immediately after the war were towards the far end of Elmdon Lane beyond the junction with Elmdon Road. The houses were built by

Thomas Davis who came from Castle Bromwich and comprised a mixture of detached and semi-detached houses. They were built on both sides of an existing 5 bedroomed house on the right hand side of Elmdon Lane called 'Ponteland' built before the war for Arnold Learner and his family.

When the new houses were built 'Ponteland' became No.164 and in 1945 my uncle Harry King moved in there with my grandmother Emily King, my aunt Emily Richards and her husband Oswald. They remained there until 1972.

The houses built by Thomas Davies each side of 'Ponteland' were numbered 156 to 162 and 166 to 186 in Elmdon Lane. He built three detached houses first, No.162 which he built for his own residence, he then built No.176 which he built for my father Edmund Crawford, my mother Winifred and myself and sister Jean. At the far end No.186 was another detached house built for Albert and Joyce Goddard. He then built two pairs of semi-detached each side of my father's house.

1950 No.176 Elmdon Lane shortly after occupation.

Mr. Davis applied for planning permission to build a second row of houses in the rear gardens, this was rejected because of the proximity of the main runway, which can be seen beyond the hedgerow. This was before the arrival of the 'bund'.

From the Davis house the two pairs of semi-detached Nos.168 to 174 were occupied by the Maxwell family, Len and Olive Troman, (Olive Troman still lives there), Bob Reid and his family and the Bowater family. The second pair of semi-detached Nos.178 to 184 were built for the Stevens, Green, Organ and Berrett families. The Berrett family emigrated to New Zealand in 1955, and having married that year, my wife Joan and I, followed them into No.184.

1950 Rear gardens of houses 176 to 186. The distance from the rear of the properties to the hedge was 170 yards and as can be seen, my father was a keen gardener.

2009 The houses built in Elmdon Lane Nos.166 to 186.

There were several other houses built by Mr. Davis on the village side of No.164 and Harold Enstone who was Headmaster of Marston Green Junior School moved into one of them.

Thomas Davis, apart from the houses in Elmdon Lane, built several houses in Coleshill Road. Two detached properties opposite Berwicks Lane were numbered 106 and 108. The original owners were the Walters family in 106 and Dave Coles in 108.

In 1966 my wife and I, with our 2 children Jeanette and Gillian moved into 106, the Walters family having moved to Water Orton. Mr. Davis also built several detached houses further up Coleshill Road past 'Gorse Farm'.

During the next two decades, the 1950s and 1960s, virtually all of the post war housing in the village itself was carried out. The largest developments were Digby Drive, Aylesford Drive, Moseley Drive and Brook Croft.

Outside of the village came the giant Chelmsley Wood complex, bringing part of Moor End Avenue and side roads Cambridge Drive and Norwich Croft into the parish boundary of Bickenhill

Further down Elmdon Lane immediately past an older house called 'Heath Heys' a new complex of houses was built in 1957/58 on open fields behind that property, existing bungalows, and further properties on the closed section of Elmdon Lane towards the Airport boundary. There were 106 properties in total, all semi-detached and the development was called Digby Drive.

2009 Digby Drive houses looking towards the village.

2009 Houses and circular island at the Airport end of Digby Drive.

There was a single detached house and 2 bungalows on the right hand side of the entrance roadway but I believe they were built later.

As mentioned earlier on the 1880 Ordnance Survey Map, an area to the left off Holly Lane opposite the junction with Chelmsley Lane, was listed as 'Allotment Gardens'.

At some time later, probably in the mid 1930s, Bob and Peter Moseley who lived in Alcott Lane bought the land and set themselves up as Nurserymen. After the war in the period 1964 to 1966 some 120 houses were built on the site and rather aptly called Moseley Drive.

2009 The approach road leading into Moseley Drive.

2009 Moseley Drive with 'Martin Rise' on the right.

To the left of the railway bridge in Land Lane there is a detached house which had a tennis court alongside (where 6 present day houses have been built below the level of the bridge approach). The family of Vic Clarke lived there, there were two sons Ken and Don, Ken was a very good footballer and was centre forward for the Marston Green team of the day, Don was called up into the Royal Air Force and having musical 'talents' played for the Air Force Band. Later, after the war the band continued, calling themselves the 'Squadronaires' and for some time in the 1950s, they were a very popular dance band. In Hall Drive there was a house called 'Hall House' which stood behind the Free Church, it was severely damaged during the war.

Sometime after the war, Hall Drive was extended and 23 new houses were built by the Howell brothers in the period 1961 to 1964, the houses were mostly semi-detached on both sides of the roadway and at the far end turned left for some 50 yards to what was open land. The houses were built in two phases, 8 houses on the right had bay windows at the front of the property, the remainder had a flatter frontage.

2009 Houses in Hall Drive taken from Land Lane.

Some two years later the Howell brothers submitted a planning application to build further houses on the open land beyond Hall Drive of similar design to those already built. As the land was of significant acreage the application was turned down as the Planning Authority wanted more houses on the site.

Another builder, Morris and Jacobs put in an alternative application to build over 100 'town houses' which was approved. The new roadway became Aylesford Drive and included 2 small 'cul de sacs' on the right hand 'Hemlingford Croft' and 'The Rise'. These houses were built in the period 1965/1966.

2009 Houses in Aylesford Drive looking towards the Elmdon Road railway bridge end.

   To the left of this junction with Hall Drive there are 3 pairs of semi-detached houses and 2 detached properties, numbering up to No.17 and thoughtfully with No.13 missing for obvious reasons.

2009 Aylesford Drive houses and lock up garages taken from the Elmdon Road railway bridge looking towards the village.

When the houses in 'Brook Croft' were built in the 1950s a strange anomaly came to light which caused some confusion. For years the 'Low Brook' had been recognised as the natural boundary between Bickenhill Parish and Coleshill Parish.

When the houses arrived, Ordnance Survey Maps of that time indicated that two of the houses were in fact half in Coleshill Parish and half in Bickenhill Parish. After much research it was found that in the Ward Book of the day, it was noted that the brook had been re-aligned in 1770 but apparently never recorded on any maps.

2009 The houses in 'Brook Croft' taken from Bickenhill Road.

Most of the properties were semi-detached but at the far end there were a couple of detached houses. As mentioned earlier, severe flooding affected the Low Brook in winter time during heavy rains. I do remember 1958 was a severe winter with deep snow falls which when the thaw took place, resulted in a number of properties having flood waters entering the front door of their houses, running through and escaping by way of the rear doors.

Fortunately, about the same time runway extensions were being carried out at Birmingham Airport, the section of Low Brook which ran across the Airport Land was culverted and the brook itself was dredged to its present depth. The expenditure for the dredging including new bridges at Coleshill Road and Bickenhill Road, amounted to £17,000 with running sand causing severe problems during the dredging.

At the same time that Brook Croft was built additional properties were built on the left hand side of Bickenhill Road on each side of Brook Croft.

Nearer to the village, three pairs of semi-detached houses and a single detached house were built numbered 20 to 32 on the left hand side of Bickenhill Road.

Past Brook Croft, two pairs of semi-detached houses were built numbered 34 to 40 and more recently in the early 2000s a large 4 bedroomed house with a separate garage was built nearer to the Brook.

Across Bickenhill Road nearer to the village than Brook Croft is 'Mowe Croft' so called because the land, owned by John Mowe a local Councillor and Magistrate, like other properties, because of many worthy activities in the village over many years the road was named after him. Apparently he sold the land to build one house in the early 1930s, but the application was turned down and he had to return the deposit. He sold the land again later to a Mr. Price who submitted a planning application to build two houses and again this application was turned down. The Council believed in preserving the 'green belt' in those days.

After the war a fresh application to build there was submitted. The Council objected but for whatever reason 16 properties were actually built. In light of the Council objection, officials from the Warwickshire Planning Department came along and said that the decision was wrong and two houses would have to be demolished to make way for a roundabout so that vehicles could turn round in the 'cul de sac'. But the houses had all been sold and the Council were then advised to let them remain.

Unbelievable – so much for the authority of Planning Administration.

The Council could have exercised their right to have had the two properties taken down but because there were 16 buyers ready to move in, the Council let it go. In fact there are lock up garages at the far end with ample space to turn round.

2009 'Mowe Croft' 4 pairs of semi-detached on both sides of roadway.

On the 1880 Ordnance Survey Map, where in the present day 'The Orchard' is situated, there used to be an old cottage which belonged to the 'Barnett' family. Miss Barnett was the Head Teacher at the first school in Marston Green located in Land Lane.

The land belonging to the Barnett's was quite extensive and ran down Bickenhill Road from the back of the school in Land Lane. The Barnett family had two sons Geoffrey and Francis, they both sang in the St.Leonard's Choir which was very successful particularly in the 1950/1960s. Geoffrey went on to sing with the Coventry Cathedral Choir for many years. Geoffrey was also an architect and designed a new house called 'The Pines' to replace the old cottage. This new house now stands by the roadway leading into the group of 11 houses named 'The Oaklands' which occupies the area where the old cottage was situated.

2009 'The Oaklands' on the right hand side of Bickenhill Road.

2009 'The Pines' former home of the Barnett family.

2009 Two pairs of semi-detached houses, Nos.11, 15, 17 and 19 right hand side of Bickenhill Road built extending down to 'The Oaklands'.

2009 Nos.2, 4 and 6, three bedroomed 'dormer' bungalows in Bickenhill Road built in the early 1970s.

No.2 has recently become L'Agence Consulate De France (Agency of the French Consultant) since the owner retired from his former employment as French Teacher at a local comprehensive school.

Between the railway bridges at Land Lane and Elmdon Road are two 'cul de sacs' on the left hand side of Elmdon Lane called Canterbury Drive and 'The Greenway'. Canterbury Drive took its name from Canterbury House which was the home of Cary Gilson the Headmaster of King Edwards VI Boys School, apparently it was demolished in the early 1920s. Later in the 1920s two semi-detached houses were built at the same place by George Foster numbered 103 and 105. At the rear of the properties was a large pit from which gravel was extracted at the time the railway was built. In the 1950/1960s the Pit was filled in and after lying remote for many years the Canterbury Drive houses were built on the site in the 1970s.

2009 Houses in Canterbury Drive leading off Elmdon Lane. The 40 houses in the 'Drive' comprise a mixture of properties, immediately on the left where the roadway turns right to run parallel to the railway, there are 2 blocks of maisonettes numbered 1 to 21. Opposite on the right are 6 detached houses followed by a row of 14 semi-detached properties, and at the far end are 6 terraced or town houses, and another 6 semi-detached properties.

Further along Elmdon Lane on the same side of the roadway is the complex called 'The Greenway' named after the family who, pre war, ran a thriving nursery business off Elmdon Road called 'Dagmar House Nurseries'. The nursery comprised several greenhouses in a large area where plants were grown and cultivated. The Greenways sold their flowers and plants in the old market hall building which was positioned on the corner of what, I believe, was called 'Church Street' opposite St.Martin's Church in the old Bull Ring which was an open market area prior to the war. Not such a large complex as most of the others built in the village more or less at the same time in the 1950 and 1960s, there are only 7 detached and 14 semi-detached.

2009 The driveway into 'The Greenway' off Elmdon Lane.

Further into the village off Chelmsley Lane next to the Doctor's Surgery is another cul de sac called 'The Orchard'. The properties were built in the 1960s and most of the

2009 Leading into the 'cul de sac' named 'The Orchard'.

16 properties are semi-detached, but it was surprising to find that at the far end to the left there is a 4 bedroomed house No.19 built as recently as 2006, and beyond the house are 2 attractive bungalows which were built in 1987.

2009 No.19 'The Orchard'.

2009 The two bungalows at the far end of 'The Orchard' cul de sac.

2009 Ivy Lodge Close at the village end of Coleshill Road provide services and offices for the Managers of Learning Disability Services in Solihull, and support giving 'Adult Shortbread Service Respite' for families and adults under the 'Solihull Care Trust'.

2009 Maisonettes built on the corner of Station Road and Land Lane, formerly the site of the old 'St.Leonard's Church' which was demolished in the late 1950s.

2009 Nos.1 to 5 Holly Lane and Nos.2 to 14 Station Road built more or less where the bowling greens and tennis courts of the old 'Tavern' public house were located. The next allocated house number is No.30 Station Road the Chartered Quantity Surveyors office. Presumably Nos.16 to 28 were allocated to the width of the 'Tavern' frontage.

2009 Eleven bungalows Nos.8 to 28 Elmdon Road. Specifically built for 'older residents of the village' in the 1960s with an age stipulation for them to be over 50.

2009 Nos.72 to 78 Station Road. These semi-detached houses were built on a vacant triangular field this side of the shops on the photograph, at the Station Road and Chelmsley Lane junction.

2009 Nos.56 and 58 Station Road. These two detached houses were built on the garden of the 'Osborne' family who had a General Grocery Store at No.58 for some 80 years. During summer months tables and chairs were laid out, and teas and light refreshments were available in the garden.

2009 Bungalows numbered 1 to 5 in Berwicks Lane.

In days gone by, long before the Chelmsley Wood complex was built, Berwicks Lane was just a rough track which continued for some half a mile, and was the recognised route to 'Alcott Hall Farm' seen on page 20.

2000 Whilst not strictly in the village, the row of semi-detached houses in Bell Lane replaced the old cottages and blacksmith's forge seen on page 166.

Chapter 24

DOCTORS, SURGERIES and CLINICS

THE FIRST residential doctor in Marston Green was I believe Dr.Honigsberger and he held his surgeries from his own house which was called 'Airport View' and if properties had been numbered in those days would have been No.110 Elmdon Lane. The house was a large 4 or 5 bedroomed house, not particularly attractive, and was 'whitewashed' or painted white externally. Dr.Honigsberger was of Austrian nationality and though a good doctor, suffered because during the war, there were a few individuals who believed that he was German, though with a name like 'Honigsberger' I would hardly have thought that was likely.

Having indicated that the house was not attractive, some time after the war a planning application to demolish it and replace it with two dwellings was rejected. It has however, since been demolished and replaced by a single large modern property.

The next doctor who opened a surgery in the village was Dr.Jenkins, his surgery was at No.66 Elmdon Lane to the right of the Land Lane junction. According to my Medical Card he was my doctor in 1950. He was well liked in the village and was very good with children.

My personal recollection of him was when I went to the surgery having a stiff neck through rowing on Ward End Park one lunch time. He always adopted a personal interest in the care of individual patients, and in my case refused to give me painkillers, but being a golfer himself insisted I met him on the Golf Course after his surgery much to my amazement. I was in considerable pain trying to hit the ball and for some time I was only hitting the ball a few yards, but surprise, surprise after 5 or 6 holes I did manage to hit the ball generally in the right direction and was hitting it further. By the time we reached the 10th hole I had forgotten my stiff neck. What a wonderful way to cure a patient!

About that time there was a lady doctor named Skitt who lived down Newlands Lane. I think she carried out home visits. Dr.Jenkins remained as the village doctor into the 1960s when he retired and moved, I think to Bournemouth. He was followed by Dr.O'Sullivan who didn't stay long, but interestingly had Patrick McGowan of the 'Avengers' as his brother in law.

Three doctors who already had a surgery in Yardley came to Marston Green in the early 1970s and opened a practice in partnership at a new surgery at No.31 in Chelmsley Lane. The three doctors were Drs.Rayton, Cutler and Khalid Rehmany with Doctor Rehmany living in Coleshill Heath Road. Later, after a short period of time, due to problems with no area suitable for 'off road' patient parking, the practice moved across the road to No.20 Chelmsley Lane.

2009 The early surgery No.31 Chelmsley Lane.

In the late 1990s Doctors Cutler and Rehmany retired and Doctor Reyton was joined by Doctor Sagoo in 1999. A short while later Doctor Reyton retired and Doctor Syed replaced him and formed a new partnership with Doctor Sagoo. The practice by this time was in need of more space, so substantial modernisation and increased capacity and extra rooms were provided to improve doctor/patient consultations in the new surgery at No.20 Chelmsley Lane. The practice also had an Advanced Nurse Practitioner Cathy Groves and a Senior Practice Nurse Sue Nightingale and Locum doctors attended from time to time.

2009 The new surgery at No.20 Chelmsley Lane.

THE LAND LANE CLINIC

The Clinic which I am sure was the first in Marston Green, opened at the same time as the Library which was back in 1958. In those early days there used to be a 'Health Visitor' and a 'District Nurse' and they were often seen calling on families with babies and also to more elderly patients.

2009 The Clinic in Land Lane.

The Clinic has grown over the years, and many other services are offered from the premises these days. Invariably, in most cases patients attending the Clinic are from Doctor's referrals at local surgeries. There are Dentists who are able to treat patients with dental problems and similarly there are Chiropodists for those requiring attention relevant to foot health. The Clinic still have nurses carrying out Health Visiting activities but this generally is in regard to babies and young children up to the age of five years.

Other services offered are Speech and Language Therapy to assist children with problems in this area and in communication difficulties. Diabetes is a subject which affects all ages and advice is available on aspects of diet and control of the problem. The Clinic is also the local hearing aid centre which mainly is for Hearing Aid battery collection. The Clinic is generally open Monday to Friday from 9.00 am. to 5.00 pm.

The District Nurses are no longer at the Clinic but have moved to the Primary Care Centre at Chelmsley Wood.

There are rooms available for short term clinics in connection with Physiotherapy, Psychiatry, T.B. and general Primary Care. It is emphasised again that most services do require a referral and an appointment.

Chapter 25

MARSTON GREEN LIBRARIES

HAVING RECENTLY achieved its 40th Anniversary, the staff of the Library in Land Lane were immensely pleased by how many villagers came along and enjoyed the tremendous array of old photographs which they had put on display, showing old farms and cottages which sadly have long since gone. Over the years, the village has celebrated Coronations, Jubilees and Festivals with 'fancy dress' parades combined with decorated floats and everyone joining in.

The presentation of photographs and written descriptions by individuals giving details of their personal memories of their days spent in the village, gave newcomers to Marston Green the opportunity to look back and read about those events in days gone by. Hopefully they would appreciate the pleasure of former village life with everyone knowing their neighbours, having local shopkeepers who provided fresh local produce and other commodities, and offered personal and friendly service not always given in today's supermarkets.

Having lived in the village for over 80 years, having experienced so many activities and witnessed the many changes that have taken place, it did bring into perspective that for virtually half of my lifetime, Marston Green did not have the convenience and facilities of a Library.

However, in earlier days there were retail properties where books could be borrowed. In the early 1930s the newsagents and stationers trading under the title of the 'Kiosk' in Station Road close to the Station, and owned by a Mr. Atack did run a Lending Library. Later in the 1940s and early 50s, at No.47 Station Road a confectioners and stationers named Rothmans offered a similar amenity. In both cases the area displaying books only occupied a small space. I have no idea where the books came from, I am aware that we did have a mobile Library service that came to the village from time to time but whether it operated before the war I am not sure.

After the war a 'temporary' arrangement to provide a Library was carried out in the old St.Leonard's Church which was located in Station Road opposite Coleshill Road junction. At that time Marston Green came under Meriden Rural District Council and the village library therefore would have been administered by the Warwickshire County Libraries. Joy Hancock from Warwickshire Libraries was the lady in charge and her written account details the problems she had to overcome. She describes the building as "very decrepit with holes in the floorboards and broken windows, with mice running around and birds in the rafters".

"The books were kept on metal shelving around the room, with wooden fronts padlocked on (these had to be removed before opening, and replaced after when closing). Returned books were put on rickety tables, and the Issue Desk was another table, and the piano was used as a shelf for requested books". Local girls, Vera Webb, Stella Reece, Jean Chance and Mrs. Mary Walker all volunteered and helped Joy Hancock. Vera Webb recalls that from time to time "a letter would be received from Warwickshire Libraries informing them when the next delivery of books would be delivered. We would then box up all the books that were to be returned, and on the appointed date someone with the key would be there to let in the delivery driver to collect the returned books and hand over the replacement books". The building was finally demolished and replaced by the present day maisonettes in the 1950s.

In the early 1960s another temporary move was made to an old Terrapin Classroom off Elmdon Lane remaining from the old school, positioned on the former playing field. Joy Hancock stated that this "was a pleasant change environmentally but there were no facilities and she appreciated the kind lady across the road who allowed her amenities to use whenever she needed a comfort break". During the time that this building was in use the old school was demolished to make way for the new Library and Clinic to be built.

Thursday October 23rd 1998 – 40th Anniversary of opening of Library.

The photograph on the previous page shows The Mayor of Solihull about to cut the Anniversary Cake. Library staff, past and present were in attendance, (from left to right) Wendy Kettle, Marie Zizzi, Evelyn Withey, Deborah Maycroft, Joy Hancock, Helen Flannery, Elaine Allen and Mayor of Solihull David Bell.

The present Library was opened in 1968 still administered by Warwickshire Libraries but in 1974 Meriden Rural District was abolished due to the Local Government Act of 1972. The Library was then transferred to the authority of Solihull Metropolitan Borough Council with overall administration from Solihull Library, with two 'job share' managers Mrs. Amanda Armstrong and Ms.Sally Cotterill.

October 2008 Present Day Library Staff. Elaine Allen, Marie Zizzi, Helen Flannery and Deborah Maycroft with section of photographic display of old Marston Green pictures seen to the left beyond them.

The new premises however have amenities significantly improved to that of the basic function of a Lending Library. Marston Green Library now offers a bright welcoming space for all ages, free internet access and numerous activities throughout the year. There is a 'bookstart bookcrawl' a joining incentive for 0 to 4 years old children. Every Monday there is an 'Under 5s' story time reading session. There are frequent school 'class visits' and 'playgroup visits'. From time to time there are displays for current village events and anniversaries, and coffee mornings are held to promote these events.

Chapter 26

SPORT IN MARSTON GREEN

FOOTBALL:

There have always been football clubs over the years, most of them playing under the name of Marston Green, but sadly with no continuity. Often a team of youngsters got together, formed a team, entered a league, not often successfully, grew old, then disbanded, to be followed by another generation of youngsters.

At some time in the early 1920s, the football pitch would have disappeared as the 'Tavern' by 1925 had laid bowling greens and tennis courts. Changing rooms were provided and a large wooden Chalet was installed at the rear of the 'Tavern' which was used for tea rooms after the various matches were played there. The Chalet was large enough to hold general meetings, club dinner dances and wedding receptions.

1919/1920 An early 'post 1st war' Marston Green team. This team played at the back of the old 'Tavern' which was open land in those days. Standing: Reg Sturmy, Pettifer, Alec Tart, Harold Wilson, H.Pettifer, Len Palmer, William Bissell (junr) and Albert Crook (senr). Seated: Henry Herriott, Joe Knight, Albert Crook, George Griffin, Alec Palmer, F.Hall and Walter Crook.

During the last war, adult teams obviously struggled with players being mobilised into the 'armed forces'. In the early days of the war, young lads in the village were always able to get a game by turning up at private grounds belonging to local companies. Like many other youngsters we all enjoyed playing competitive football in these works league games and we decided to form our own team and we joined a league called the Birmingham J.O.C. Under 18s. The team was reasonably successful and had some good local lads playing but also suffered with player availability.

In 1942, discussions took place with another team of lads from the Sheldon area who were similarly beset with the same problem of not enough players. They decided to amalgamate and started playing under the banner of Marston Green. From that point on they never looked back and in the 1943/1944 season they played brilliantly and were a match for any team.

They won the League Championship, they also won 2 Cups, the 'Norman Chamberlain Cup' and the 'Birmingham Football Club Cup'. In the whole of the season, they lost just one game and won the League Championship convincingly. Both of the Cup Finals were played at Villa Park and there was tremendous support from locals who travelled to the matches.

Two of the players, Albert Ensor from Shustoke, and Harry Marriott from Sheldon both scored over 50 goals during the season, several of the team were offered trials with local clubs, Aston Villa, Birmingham and West Bromwich Albion. Ensor did turn out for the Albion in a number of games and Marriott later played in the Birmingham Combination League in semi-professional football.

However, like other teams before them, several of the players soon became lost to the team due to recruitment into the Armed Forces, and whilst in theory the team continued, they never aspired to such performances again.

Marston Green Football Club 1943/44. Standing at rear: Bill Rogers, Harold Wilson, George Taylor and Fred Davis. Centre: Roy Davis, Jock Philips, Ben Brewer, Ken Pemberton, John Ides, Les Horton and Graham Crawford. Front: John Harris, Ron Wilson, 'Moggie' Morrison (capt), Albert Ensor, Harry Marriott and Norman Robson.

In the 1930s, the team of the day had several excellent players, Norman Bowker, Ken Sugarman, Ken Clark, Bill Shufflebotham, all played for the league team. Norman Bowker was on Birmingham's books. Ken Greenway, Dennis Webb, and Norman Docker played regularly and the team more than held their own against most teams.

After the war ended, football resumed at the Recreation Ground but many of the pre war team did not return for various reasons, the saddest being Norman Bowker who lost his life in an air crash in Canada, having survived many bombing flights over enemy territory during the war.

Another team which came along were Marston United. They were local lads who formed a team and were the first team to play Sunday football. Sunday football was not allowed in pre war days, but because everyone had to work on Saturdays a League was formed which legitimised the problem, having the wonderful title of 'Birmingham Monday League – Sunday Section'.

At first they had moderate success, but the end of the war helped to give improved performances as players returned from service with the 'armed forces'. They improved as better players came along and in the 1951/1952 season they won the prestigious 'Wheeler Cup' played at St.Andrews. In the final they played a 'pub team' despite their title 'Witton Allotments', they regularly won the league championship and were

1948/1949 Marston Green Football Club. Back Row: Harry Lee, Harry Mellish, Bill Shufflebotham, Gerald Brazier, Bill Brazier, Paddy Agnew, (?), Don Brazier, Ernie Wyatt, Harold Wilson and unknown Referee. Front Row: Ken Sugarman, Ken Greenway, Dennis Webb, Bill Talbot, Taffy Powell and Bob Lewis.

known to include professional players from the Birmingham League in their team, as did a lot of the 'pub teams'.

The final was well supported by local villagers, and despite going twice behind, Marston United to draw 2-2 with a late equaliser. The game was played in the evening, and as floodlights had not been introduced in those days, the result stood as a draw, and the Cup was shared having 6 months each. Marston United won the toss and were therefore able to bring the Cup back to Marston Green to celebrate with their supporters.

1948/49 Early Marston United Football Club. Back Row: Gerald White, Walter Hazeldene, Richard Clarke, Fred Davis, John Hutchison, Les Thompson, Edgar Evans, Roy Thompson and Keith Ollerenshaw.
Centre: Sid Cross, Tom Warman, Roy Davis, Eddie Crawford and Graham Crawford. Front: Norman Yates, Walter Curley, Doug Lewis, Alan Clements and

Bernard Phipps. For information: Sid Cross was the British Triple Jump Champion entered in the 1948 Olympics – we had to drop him.

1951/52 Marston United Football Club.
Standing: Les Thompson, Gerald Brazier, Roy Davis, John Hutchison, Graham Crawford, Don Brazier and Tom Warman.
Seated: Harry Gillard, Philip Morris, Roy Thompson, Eric Wootton (Capt), Bill Talbot and Alan Clements.

CRICKET:

Marston Green Cricket Club was formed in 1926, and there have been many changes that have affected the Club since then. The Club has moved around the village, and the Recreation Ground Headquarters are the fourth location at which the Club has played. In 1926, cricket was only played on Saturdays, and all games were played as 'friendlies', there were no leagues around at that time.

The first ground was off Elmdon Road, at a field more or less where Hidcote Grove is now situated. There was then a move across the village to Elmdon Lane at 'Chapel House Farm' which later became Marston Green Municipal Golf Course. I was told that neither of these were really acceptable and a third move was made to a field at the back of the 'Bell Inn' roughly where 'Whitesmore School' was built after the war.

In 1937 the Recreation Ground was laid out and the following year the Club made their fourth and last move there, they brought their old wooden pavilion that had moved from ground to ground with them. The facilities were primitive, there was no

1926 Marston Green Cricket Club, first official photo taken at Chapel House Farm.
Standing: John Heron, Ray Watkins, Roger Ward, Norman Wilson, Norman Pugh, Arthur Morrison, Hugh Arton (Capt), Louis Couzens, Ralph Clift, Henry Heath and John Currall.
Squatting: Fred Gilman, Robert Couzens, Peter Arton and Pat Flanagan.

water on site, there was no kitchen as such, food had to be prepared on trestle tables that were also used to lay out the meals for at least 26 people. Water had to be fetched from the 'Durex Abrasives' ground (later the 3Ms) on a hand trailer carrying a dustbin full of water. A 'Calor Gas' cylinder was used to boil the water for making tea.

During wartime the Club relied heavily on guest players and young lads in the village often managed to get into the team at an earlier age than normally expected. Not strictly a guest player was Doug Cotton who lived in Coleshill Road, but came to the village because he, being a pilot was seconded to Elmdon Airport, as it was in those days. Subsequently, during the war he piloted the 'Stirling' bombers which were being assembled at the 'shadow' factory at what is now known as the Elmdon Trading Estate. John Brookes and Ron Wilkinson also worked at the Airport.

The most interesting recruit was a young airman named Bernard Constable. Bernard took many wickets as a fast bowler for the Club, but after the war went into county cricket as a top order batsman for the Surrey side that won the County Championship for seven successive seasons. It didn't say much for the Marston Green Club selectors as 'talent spotters', because Bernard regularly exceeded a 1000 runs for Surrey in a side which included Peter

1935 Marston Green Cricket Club. Fancy dress match on Monday 6th May to commemorate 'Silver Jubilee' of King George V and Queen Mary. Photograph taken at rear of the 'Bell Inn'.
Back Row: Eddie Briers, Len Anderton, Peter Arton, Norman Wallace, Ernie Walters, Eddie Moseley, Arthur Crane, Gordon Corbett, Reg Moseley, Roger Ward, Hugh Arton, Frank Pemberton (Senr) and Stan Metcalfe. Centre: Mary Wilson, Mary Anderton, Hilda Crane, Jon Owens (Robert on lap), Charles Moseley (Robin in front), (?) (?), Mrs. Dalman, Mrs. Metcalfe and Barbara Wyatt. Front Row: Robert Metcalfe, (?) Ron Pemberton, (?) Peter Pemberton and (?).

1942 Wartime Cricket at Marston Green. Rear: John Owens, Eddie Moseley, Harold Dean, Doug Cotton, John Brookes and John Summers (Secretary). Centre: George Taylor, Ron Wilkinson, Frank Pemberton (Chairman), Tom Betts (Captain), and Ron Brindley. Front: Bill Rogers (Umpire), Peter Troy (Scorer) and Reg Moseley.

1948 Marston Green First XI. Rear: Bill Rogers (Umpire), Eddie Moseley, Doug Cotton, George Kay, Graham Crawford and unknown umpire. Centre: Frank Greenway, Tom Betts (Captain), Ray Essam and Doug Stevens. Front: Richard Clarke, Bill Talbot and Neville Roden.

May, Ken Barrington, Jim Laker and Tony Lock all who represented the England team for many years.

Having previously mentioned the difficulty of transporting water from the neighbouring sports ground of the 3Ms, the Club obtained permission from the Parish Council to lay a water main from the Toilets which used to stand at the bottom Coleshill end of the Recreation Ground. Local farmer Harry Musson, also a member of the Club, dug the trench with a digger powered by a tractor, we had 'professional' expertise amongst members, a couple of plumbers, who carried out the piping system which made tea preparation much easier, not to mention the advantage of water for the square in dry summers.

For many years, the Club had managed with the old wooden building as the Pavilion, but sadly we had problems with it being vulnerable to vandalism. On one occasion three youths attempted to smash down the double doors using the club's heavy roller as a weapon. Fortunately, they were spotted and held until the Police arrived. They were taken to court, were found guilty and were sentenced to be detained in a young offenders establishment. Surprise, surprise, they never served any time because every establishment was full.

Because of this the club had no alternative but to remove the lower timber at the front and replace with a brick frontage which solved the problem at that time. Despite our efforts, ever increasing remedial repairs became too frequent. At that time the Parish council began to express concern at the shabby appearance of not only the Pavilion but also an old army Nissen hut which stood at the rear of the Pavilion which the Football Club used as their changing room. Both clubs were forever indebted to the Parish Council as they decided to build a brick structure to cater for both clubs.

The building was built at a cost of £8,000 but the clubs had to contribute £1,000. We were fortunate that Graham Hankinson and I, both had joined the Council to hurry up long time discussions regarding a new Pavilion. We

1962 Marston Green First XI. Rear: Richard Blakey, Richard Clarke, Derek Wilson, Don Barber, John Maund and Eric Barnett. Front: Hugh Willey, Barry Rose, Graham Crawford (Captain), Dudley Ward, Jack Rawlins and Mark Anderton (Scorer).

represented the Council on the Warwickshire National Playing Fields Association and were granted £4,000 towards the cost due to its dual purpose activity. The grant was the largest ever given.

Because the Club had progressed from operating from a much travelled wooden pavilion to the new Council owned multi purpose pavilion, the Club were able to attract better players. For many years an Annual Dinner Dance had been held albeit not always well attended. At the function a well known local was invited to be Guest of Honour from various activities, prominent local district councillors, Warwickshire County cricketers, foreign test players turning out for Warwickshire, local professional footballers and a local tennis player who lived in the village and had appeared at Wimbledon. Unfortunately the Club did have disappointments when our 'guest' was sometimes 'otherwise engaged' often at the last moment.

At that time before league cricket was introduced, fixtures were arranged mainly against local clubs and were classed as 'friendlies'. It was decided to solve the problem associated with finding a 'guest of honour' and present a Cup each year to the 'Local Outstanding Cricketer of the Year' who would be invited to be our 'Guest'. The local newspaper at that time was the Coleshill Chronicle, and each week they printed comprehensive results of all the local cricket matches which solved the problem of who to choose. This trophy was awarded for 31 years which did bring in much interest and we believed, engendered a 'friendlier' relationship between clubs.

Year	Award Winners and Home Club
1961	R.J.Morris of Coleshill Cricket Club
1962	R.Kings of Nether Whitacre Cricket Club
1963	J.Day of Water Orton Cricket Club
1964	J.Willetts of Water Orton Cricket Club
1965	P.Atkins of Water Orton Cricket Club
1966	A.W.James of Coleshill Cricket Club
1967	F.S.Appleyard of Water Orton Cricket Club
1968	R.D.Norris of Tamworth Cricket Club
1969	F.Baird of Nether Whitacre Cricket Club
1970	G.Davies of Atherston Cricket Club
1971	M.Price of Water Orton Cricket Club
1972	D.J.W.Deamer of Lloyds Bank Cricket Club.
1973	M.Mason of Four Oaks Saints Cricket Club
1974	D.Woodhead of Solihull Municipal Cricket Club
1975	G.Buckley of Marston Green Cricket Club
1976	G.E.Crawford of Marston Green Cricket Club
1977	D.J.A.Winter of Solihull Municipal Cricket Club
1978	J.Griffiths of Wishaw Cricket Club
1979	D.Poletti of Water Orton Cricket Club
1980	D.J.W.Deamer of Lloyds Bank Cricket Club
1981	D.J.A.Winter of Solihull Municipal Cricket Club

1982   R.Cox of Marston Green Cricket Club
1983   R.Jenkins of Leek Wootton Cricket Club
1984   M.L.A.Anderton of Marston Green Cricket Club
1985   M.Cook of Corley Cricket Club
1986   D.Hart of Sheldona Marlboro Cricket Club
1987   R.J.Longhorne of Four Oaks Saints Cricket Club
1988   F.S.Williams of Leek Wootton Cricket Club
1989   R.Long of Four Oaks All Saints Cricket Club
1990   S.Perryman of Marston Green Cricket Club
1991   A.L.Gordon of Coleshill Cricket Club

League Cricket took over Club Cricket and they arranged the fixtures which in effect brought an end to years of mutually arranged matches against local clubs.

It was about the same time that Club cricket changed for ever, having had a basic alliance to friendly cricket for probably 50 or 60 years. League cricket came into the game, which it must be said, was not wholeheartedly supported by all cricketers.

Marston Green up to the time of the new Pavilion, could not have stood any chance of entering a league, purely because new guide-lines were set for admittance to leagues.

The size of grounds were set to minimum yardages, matches were to be off fixed length of innings – 50

1972 The official opening of the new Pavilion at the Recreation Ground with Graham Hankinson, Chairman of the Bickenhill Parish Council, congratulating the Architect Mr. Meredith with members of the Parish Council in attendance. Left to right: Len Martin, Kate Bloor, Janice Billingham, Henry Heath, Leah Martin, Robert Cooper, Jim Whitham, Graham Billingham, Graham Crawford, Mr. Meredith, Graham Hankinson and Peter Barrie.

overs each was the norm, paid neutral umpires were demanded, new balls for every innings, match score sheets to be submitted to Leagues to be received within 48 hours, and results phoned to the local newspaper (Birmingham Mail) straight away after the game.

Marston Green had missed out on all of this. League cricket effectively brought an end to some 50 to 60 years of 'friendly' cricket which had the idealistic intention of clubs playing each other in an enjoyable and sporting atmosphere, and where the result of the match was not important. I don't believe anyone accepted that. To lose a 'local' derby against your immediate neighbouring club meant that you had lost 'bragging rights' in your local pubs until the next season.

The club had little alternative but to accept league cricket and after discussions with like minded clubs it was decided to form another league. The name of the league was the Mercian Club Cricket league and the original clubs were Birch Coppice,

1976 Marston Green First XI. Taken at Lye Cricket Club following their victory which gave them the Championship of the Mercian Club Cricket League. Rear: David Denstone, Colin Whitehouse, John Evans, Martin Hill, Graham Crawford, David Anderton and Bob Hill (Umpire). Front: Graham Buckley, Mark Anderton, Lance Anderton (Capt), Keith Carpenter, Richard Ward and Wendy Preston (Scorer).

Dunlop Sports, Erdington Court, Four Oaks Saints, Hammerwich, Lea Marston, Marston Green, Old Moselians, Tipton, Walsall Trinity, Walsall Wood and Wilnecote. There were two Divisions with promotion and relegation.

The Club enjoyed considerable success in League Cricket and we hosted night games against Birmingham League teams, against Warwickshire Cricket Club in support of individual player's benefits. One was against Andy Lloyd who captained the Club for a few years. The most notable however was when we were fortunate to get Alvin Kallicharran the West Indian test player to turn out in a Warwickshire team in 1983. There was a good crowd who came along, we had a collection for him which raised £310 and he attended the Club Dinner Dance as Guest of Honour.

Because of the requirements for minimum yardages of grounds, and because there was a need for 40 yards to be at least behind the wickets the Club had to get permission from Bickenhill Parish Council to remove the hedge which ran the full length

1982 International Cricket at Marston Green. The 'historic' occasion when the Club entertained 'Papua New Guinea' in a warm up game for the 1982 Cricket World Cup. Rear: Bob Hill (Treasurer), John Clark, Steve Williams, Ron Hughes, Harry Musson (President), Colin Stanley, Graham Crawford (Secretary), Eric Barnett (Chairman). Front: Ron Cox, Mark Anderton, Martin Hill, David Mullard, Steve Mullard (Captain), Lance Anderton, Steve Eaton and David Hill. Gary Anderton (Scorer) squatting.

1983 Harry Musson the Club President, presented an inscribed tankard to Alvin Kallicharran and a cheque was handed over for his benefit fund.

from the car park up to the Groundsman's House. This gave a satisfactory distance. Another requirement called for wicket covers and site screens at both ends, which at the Bickenhill Road end caused problems due to the slope from the wicket down to the fence. The Papuan game referred to was the start of a tremendous run of success for the Club, in that year they won the Championship of the League again and two knock out trophies. A new 'pyramid' the Central Warwickshire League started which meant even more league games.

In 1984 the Club successes went on, both 1st XI and 2nd XIs won the Saturday and Sunday League Championships, the 1st XI won all four knock out competitions that they entered. The Club also won the 'Team of the Year Award' presented by Solihull Sports Council. In 1985 and 1986 the Club were again double League Champions. Because of the enjoyment and friendship engendered in the earlier Papuan game, Marston Green were invited to play them again.

Papua batted first and scored a creditable 237 off their alloted overs, the Marston Green fielders excelled themselves taking 9 catches with the spinners Richard Ward and Mark Anderton taking 7 wickets between them. T.Vai 57, and Raki Ali 46 were the leading Papua batsmen. Opening batsman Graham Buckley scored a valuable 77 and Captain Steve Mullard lead by example with 86, adding 91 with Buckley and 65 with Ron Hughes in the run chase which gave Marston Green a 4 wicket win.

PAPUA INNINGS

K.Au	ct Mullard	b Hill	9
T.Vai	ct Hill	b M.Anderton	57
B.Harry	ct L.Anderton	b M.Anderton	14
W.Maha	ct Buckley	b M.Anderton	21
Raki Ila	ct Mullard	b Ward	46
C.Amini	ct Griffiths	b Ward	25
Api Laka	ct Hughes	b Ward	0
D.Lohai	ct L.Anderton	b Ward	15
Ranagi Ila	not out		20
G.Ravu		b Hill	0
L.Manu	ct Mullard	b Lomas	21
	Extras		9
		TOTAL	237

FALL OF WICKETS:
1/29, 2/72, 3/98, 4/131, 5/171, 6/171, 7/192, 8/197, 9/201, 10/237

Bowling:	*O*	*M*	*R*	*W*
David Hill	12	5	33	2
Brian Lomas	9	0	45	1
Ron Hughes	12	0	58	0
Mark Anderton	10	3	40	3
Richard Ward	9	1	54	4

MARSTON GREEN INNINGS

Ron Cox	ct K.Au	b G.Ravu	20
Graham Buckley	ct K.Au	b L.Manu	77
John Griffiths	ct D.Lohia	b G.Ravu	0
Lance Anderton	ct K.Au	b Raki Ila	7
Steve Mullard	run out		86
Brian Lomas	ct K.Au	b W.Maha	0
Ron Hughes	not out		27
David Hill	not out		4
Colin Stanley	did not bat		
Richard Ward	did not bat		
Mark Anderton	did not bat		
	Extras		18
	TOTAL for 6 wkts		239

FALL OF WICKETS:
1/53, 2/55, 3/74, 4/165, 5/166, 6/231

Bowling:	*O*	*M*	*R*	*W*
G.Ravu	12	6	13	2
C.Amimi	11	2	46	0
R.Ali	12	2	44	1
B.Harry	5	0	29	0
W.Maha	10	0	54	0
L.Manu	9	2	36	1

2009 The Cricket Ground with the Pavilion and the Caretaker's House beyond.

The appointment of a full time Groundsman and Caretaker by Bickenhill Parish Council was a wise move for many reasons, security was certainly one of them as 'break ins' had already taken place at the new pavilion. The groundsman duties apart from maintenance of the Recreation were extended to the village itself which included the Memorial Garden, the Pleck area at the corner of Coleshill Road and Bickenhill Road, where flower beds were introduced and regularly planted. The Burial Ground and the former 3Ms Sports Ground were taken over and extra football pitches came under the Council control. More recently, the ground floor of the Pavilion has been modified to provide an Office for a full time Council Clerk.

On the cricket scene, International Cricket returned to the Recreation Ground when a 'Golden Oldies' Competition took place with many countries entering teams of 'veteran cricketers' (over 65 I believe). Marston Green were fortunate enough to host

George Aston (Chairman) tossing the coin up between the two Captains to decide who batted first. I made sure there was fair play.

a match between veterans from Australia and New Zealand. They played a 50 over match which did bring along some locals who were intrigued and there were a few youngsters who turned up with autograph books hoping to see famous cricketers. I doubt if they found any.

The Australian team comprised mainly of cricketers who play in Interstate Cricket Leagues of reasonable standard but at a lower level than their established test players play, more or less equivalent to our County teams.

The New Zealand team who play their cricket along similar lines to the 'Aussies' however they did have a 'celebrity' playing for them. The wicketkeeper was a very active 75 years old and his name was Le Mesurier, cousin of John Le Mesurier, the kindly, often bewildered Sergeant, and Uncle to 'stupid boy' in T.V.s Dad's Army.

GOLFING:

Marston Green Municipal Golf Course opened as a 9 hole golf course shortly after the end of the 1939/1945 War, early in 1948 with Bill Adwick as the Professional. Bill came from 'North of the Border', was quietly spoken and could be described as a 'dour' Scot. But as a teaching professional he was highly regarded, and there have been many, many good golfers around who have fond memories of the excellent tuition (me included) that they received from Bill in those Marston Green days.

The early holes were at the rear of Chapel House Farm and extended towards Sheldon, running parallel with the railway embankment at Marston Green Station. Later the course became 18 holes and an exhibition match was played between Bill Adwick and Jack Cawsey the Pype Hayes Professional and two leading amateurs of the day Carl Bretherton and Duncan Sutherland. The enlarged course extended from the houses in Elmdon Lane towards the Airport and became a fine test of golf.

Unfortunately, runway extensions over a number of years saw a gradual demise of golf at Marston Green, most of the new holes disappeared in the early '60s and the course returned to 9 hole again. Roger Thompson who had taken over from Bill Adwick moved to a new course at Hatchford Brook, and David Owen became Professional. It remained as a 9 hole for a few years but finally passed into history some time in the 1970s. At the end of the runway Sheldon Country Park now occupies the area where some 6 holes would have been.

The intention of building a golf course was talked about in pre war days and work had started with Harry Monkhouse as Greenkeeper. Towards the end of the war meetings were held to continue to prepare the course. A copy of an earlier meeting is shown below:

❖

REPORT OF THE BOARD OF GREENKEEPING RESEARCH
14th April 1944

MARSTON GREEN GOLF COURSE

This course is not actually open for play yet having been constructed just before the war. It has been the policy to keep the greens mown and to graze as many fairways as possible to control growth. The greens fall roughly into two groups, the first represented by greens 11,13,14,15,16 and 18. The second group is greens 1,2,4,5,6,7 and 8. In the first group the growth is soft, heavy, and there is a good deal of buttercup, annual meadow grass and worms are common. In the second group, the turf is finer, there is more bent, much less weed though unfortunately, there is a tendency to be rather on the acid side. The 10th green is rather different from both groups, the right hand side conforms to the first group whilst the left is exceedingly acid, very mossy and has a thin soil. It is not recommended that any dressings should be given to the greens this year, they should be kept regularly mown as at present, and as far as it possible rosette weeds should be picked out as time permits. Much trouble however, is being caused by shrapnel from the local range. The surrounds to the greens should be kept down with the Allan Scythe, the grass to be raked up and removed.

There were two more sheets to this report looking into post war development and regular progress meetings were held over the next 4 years prior to the opening.

Following those early meetings, preparation to construct the course continued. In 1939 a Clerk of Works was appointed named Harry Monkhouse. He and his family lived in Chapel House Farm, and he acting in his capacity as Clerk of Works carried on throughout the war years tending to the 'yet to be opened' golf course. This work mainly comprised mowing and treating the greens with appropriate fertilisers as directed.

The local newspaper of the day was the 'Coleshill Chronicle' and a report published in February 1953 related the story of Mr. Monkhouse who spent the war years preparing a golf course which did not open until 1948.

14 YEARS AT GOLF COURSE

When Chapel House Farm, Marston Green was being converted into a municipal golf course in 1939, Mr. Henry Monkhouse came from Birmingham in the role of Clerk of the Works. He is still there some 14 years after, but as Head Greenkeeper. Chapel House Farm is of Tudor origin and is built on the site of an old chapel which was said to be a resting place for monks passing from Maxstoke Priory to Olton. How strangely apt that a Monkhouse should occupy what was a monk's house.

CAME FROM LICKEY Mr. Monkhouse was previously at Lickey Hills municipal golf course. Under his supervision the Marston Green course has been extended from the original 9 holes to the full 18 and has become as fine a test of golf skill as any in the golfing area.

Mr. Monkhouse in fact stayed well after the 14 years, as the newspaper article stated and he remained until he reached retirement age in the early 1960s. Similarly the article pointed out that the course was a good test of golf skill. The first 9 holes which extended from the rear of the Elmdon Lane houses were probably tougher than the second 9 holes. The first hole was a good driving hole with a slight draw to the right, and the tee shot had to drive over a bunker to reach the fairway which would give a good line into the green. It was the longest hole on the first nine and a low stroke index. The 4th hole was another sweeping fairway with rough on the right up to the green. Hole 5 was an interesting short hole needing to cross the hatchford brook in front of the green. Hole 6, another hard hole going right out to the Sheldon extremity of the course.

No.7 was a severe dog leg to the left, with a drive about 160 yards to pass high hedges and trees to give a sight of the green, unless you were tall enough and brave enough to drive over the hedge. Hole 8 was the hardest hole on the front nine, out of bounds for some 200 yards on the right, a long hit drive could get into an extensive hollow past the out of bounds and gave you a mid iron shot into the green. The last hole was a low iron shot on to a well bunkered green.

Hole 10 was a short hole to a 'postage stamp' green right alongside the platforms at the station, it was an intimidating drive due to rail passengers waiting to give you a cheer if you made a mess of it. Hole 11 was a good hole, a raised tee required a good drive to cross the brook where it passed towards the railway arches on the Birmingham side of the station. A sliced drive finished on the railway bank. Hole 12 was a short 4 hole with a well bunkered fairway. The 'dell hole' 13 needed a drive to the left, tee to green in a straight line was over a deep sunken area with plenty of trees to catch a wayward drive. 14 a short hole , 15 needed 2 good straight hits to the green. Hole 16 was the hardest hole on the return half with hedges and bunkers which could cause trouble. The last two holes were both par 5s, 17 was longest on the course, hedges on a drive length often caught off line drives which made life difficult. Hole 18 was certainly the most interesting. The drive had to cross the 'hatchford brook' about 160 yards from the tee, the next shot was all uphill over a grassy bank some 20 feet above the fairway level. If you managed those two shots it needed a chip shot on to the green with out of bounds at the rear. Otherwise it was a hard hole.

MARSTON GREEN MUNICIPAL GOLF COURSE B 2^33

Competition MONTHLY MEDAL   Date 12 – 7 – 54

Player G. E. CRAWFORD   Handicap 11

Marker's Score	Hole	Length (yds.) Gents	Ladies	Bogey	Stroke Index	Score	Net Score	Win + Lose – Half O
	1	432	346	4	5	6		
	2	360	333	4	11	4		
	3	294	286	4	13	5		
	4	423	410	4	3	4		
	5	170	110	3	15	3		
	6	425	412	5	7	5		
	7	328	300	4	9	5		
	8	406	349	4	1	5		
	9	168	156	3	17	2		
	Out	3004	2702	35		39		

Marker's Score	Hole	Length (yds.) Gents	Ladies	Bogey	Stroke Index	Score	Net Score	Win + Lose – Half O
	10	156	121	3	18	3		
	11	329	273	4	6	4		
	12	281	234	4	14	4		
	13	371	323	4	4	4		
	14	171	130	3	16	4		
	15	368	305	4	10	4		
	16	401	336	4	2	4		
	17	517	437	5	12	5		
	18	452	425	5	8	5		
	In	3046	2584	36		37		
	Out	3004	2702	35		39		
	Total	6050	5286	71		76		

Handicap   11

Net Score   65

In Medal Competitions, use Col. 7

In Bogey   " " " 7, 8 and 9

In Stableford   " " " 7 and 9

In Alliance   " " " 7 and 8

Competitor's Signature G. E. Crawford

Marker's Signature C. H. Merritt

STANDARD SCRATCH SCORE - 70

P36680– B4 (a) R 1431/26

1960 The 11th fairway looking across the 'hatchford brook' with the railway embankment (out of bounds) on the right. The buildings beyond the green were of the 'Lucas' factory that was there at that time. The tee for the last hole, the 18th was adjacent to the 11th green behind the trees on the left, and the fairway ran parallel to the 10th, over the brook and continued up hill, over a grassy bank and on to an elevated green with out of bounds behind, near to the farm buildings.

1960 Taken from the Car Park off Elmdon Lane looking towards the original Locker Room and small Tea Room which supplied tea, coffee, cool drinks, sandwiches, biscuits and cakes. The wall on the right was formed by using stone sleepers from the laying of the original track of the railway.

LAWN TENNIS:

Marston Green Lawn Tennis was founded in 1923 but in those days were known as 'Elite Lawn Tennis Club'. The photograph below was the first photograph of the Club membership with some 30 of those early players present. The dress code, especially of the ladies, recalls that of vintage tennis at Wimbledon with the long flowing dresses, and 'shorts' for the men in those days was unthinkable.

1923 The first official photograph of the 'Elite Lawn Tennis Club'.

An interesting point regarding the membership at that time shows that the ladies outnumbered the gentlemen significantly, how many 'local' sports clubs were around in those days which actually catered for ladies and gave them an opportunity to play?

Another early photograph taken in 1926 and significant change at the time gave the information that the Club was 'now' known as Marston Green L.T.C.

Marston Green males in those days did have a football club and I have been told that there was an early rugby team that also played in the village.

Quite recently, the Clubhouse has been extensively refurbished, which is now half brick and half timber with the wooden part housing the lounge section. The early wooden section has been there since 1923.

1926. Elite L.T.C. now known as Marston Green L.T.C. How many here are in the 1923 photograph?

To answer the question, I believe there was only one. The young lady in the dark dress on the later photograph 'could' be sitting in the centre row, five from the right on the 1923 photograph.

However, the 1926 photograph appears to show a much younger age group to those in the earlier photograph. Does this group indicate that a 'junior section' had been introduced to the Club.

The next photograph was taken in the early 1930s. My father did start playing about that time and I used to go with him and my mother who both played tennis. My recollections of those days were not extensive, but I do remember that there were just two grass courts, the pavilion was of timber construction with small changing rooms. There were no services laid on, no electricity, no water and the toilets were an antiquated chemical type which had to be emptied from time to time.

Not being aware of such matters then, like security, my friends and I were inquisitive enough to know that when the chemical toilet was away for emptying and cleaning, it was possible to crawl through the vacant aperture and gain admittance up into the changing rooms.

Tennis Club members taken approximately about 1930. Back row: Len (?), and Arthur Deeming. Centre: Gertrude Knight, Elsie Palmer, Les Thompson and Eric Rogers. Kneeling; Ciss Knight. Front: Gladys Anderton, Joe Knight and Kath Blunt.

Some interesting observations with this photograph. Joe Knight appeared on a 1919/1920 football team photograph earlier in the book. As he was much younger then, this photograph would suggest that he would have been about 28 years old when it was taken.

Ciss Knight I believe was his wife, she was Ciss Dalman, before she married. Co-incidently on a school photograph of 1921 she was in the rear row next to Winnie Palmer, whilst her sister

Elsie Palmer is one of the members on this photograph. They were two of the three daughters of the then Station Master of 1925, and they can be seen with their mother Mrs. Florence Palmer, and their other sister Rene sitting outside the Station Master's House which was closely adjacent to the main London to Birmingham railway line. They can be seen in the section headed 'The Railway'.

I knew most of the other people on the photograph, I grew up with the sons of Les Thompson, and the children of Gladys Anderton.

My father Edmund Crawford became quite a good player in the early 1930s and was the winner of the Men's Singles Championship in 1936.

The group shown alongside I understand were the finalists of the various Championships in 1936. In the front were my father, Edmund Crawford the Men's Singles Champion, and Edie Banner the Ladies' Singles Champion. Behind were Ray Crook and Rex Hanson who were the Men's Doubles Champions.

The other gentleman on the right, named Walter Cursley lost to my father in the Singles Final, the two ladies, Brenda Watkins on the left and Gladys Cursley on right were the Ladies Doubles Champions.

1936 DINNER DANCE

Ladies' Singles Champion Edie Banner, receiving her trophy from the Club President Elvin Morrison and alongside her is Edmund Crawford the Men's Singles Champion. On right are David Vaughton and Brenda Watkins the Mixed Doubles Champions. Other members in the photograph: Front extreme right, Helen and Ray Crook, behind them Mary and Geoffrey Barnett, at the back Irene and Ray Watkins. Front

extreme left: Mr. and Mrs. Arnold Learner, behind them Frank and Thelma Cooper. In the rear on the left: Eric Rogers, Stan Banner, Ernie Davies with M.G.L.T.C. badge behind him, and James Barnett. In the centre to the left of Elvin Morrison: Muriel Hanson and Ralph Clifford. Behind David Vaughton: Mary Davis, part hidden Mrs. Talamo and Mrs. Barnett, parents of Mary and Geoffrey Barnett.

1960
Marston Green L.T.C. took first prize in the village float competition with the theme 'Tennis through the ages'

Marston Green for many years had regular carnival processions through the village when local farmers, butchers and various organisations entered their floats to the parade. For the Tennis Club to take first prize was an admirable performance. Rosie Smythe in the centre seems to be enjoying herself – for closer inspection of her 'dated' attire see below left.

1960 Rosie Smythe in her 'so called' 1880 styling which is rather surprising as Ladies did not play at Wimbledon until 1884. The doorway shown is no longer in use but in those days was the exit from the Clubhouse.

1965 Prize winning day at the Tennis Club. The particular winners collecting their trophies were the Ladies' Double Champions nearest the camera, Betty Hiam and Betty Dight. Others in the photograph were John Boswell behind Betty Hiam, Anne Murray beyond Betty Dight, Jim Murray (long time early local dentist) with curly hair at the back, Jo and John Huddlestone, Jim Lomasney at the rear behind Rosie and Bert Smythe.

1968 Annual Dinner Dance at the 'Wheatsheaf Inn' with season's prizewinners. Left to right: John Buswell, John Huddleston (Captain), Anne Murray, Jim Lomasney (Chairman), Jo Huddleston, Betty Dight, Jim Murray, Ian Grieg and Alan Brownhill.

Marston Green L.T.C. has always been a popular and at times a very successful Club with some very good players. To pick out individuals would certainly be unfair to many others who have carried out excellent service over the years and to others who have brought credit to the good name of the Club.

Two members however, are worthy of mention quite apart from their undoubted tennis knowledge and capabilities. Sadly, neither of them are still with us, but so many recollections of happy and memorable experiences from both of them will live long in the memories of those who were involved with them over the years.

The first was Jim Lomasney who since the war years, probably did more for the Club than most others. Jim earned a reputation as a first class coach, particularly with the youngsters, and it is difficult to remember over the years, when Jim was not at the

Club and of course being actively involved. The Club web site citation indicated that Life Member Jim Lomasney, coached more children and adults than anyone else known. He was an energetic man with many talents, besides coaching tennis, he was involved with local youth clubs, football and many other sports. He was Chairman of

the Marston Green L.T.C. from 1964 to 1981. He instigated the club bar and was pleased to be able to personally pour the first pint.

Jim also officiated at Wimbledon, the highlight being picked as the net court judge in the 1975 Men's Singles final between Jimmy Connors and Ken Rosewall. Sadly Jim passed away on Wednesday 26th January 2005 at the grand old age of 91.

The second member worthy of mention was Rosie Smythe. Rosie was an inspiration to anyone who wishes to play tennis well into their retirement. Small in stature, but huge in everything else, her ability, her encouragement to others, her enthusiasm for the game and most amaz-

1999 Jim Lomasney visits his old umpiring ground – Wimbledon. Fred Perry statue plays on behind him.

ingly she managed to play reasonable tennis into her 80s. Rosie became a legend at the Club and her presence is still sorely missed today. Sadly, she passed away in 2008 at the wonderful age of 95 years.

At the age of 90 years Rosie had a memorable meeting with Ann Haydon-Jones, a local Birmingham girl who achieved national tennis fame by winning the Ladies' Singles Championship at Wimbledon in 1969. Rosie, at that age went onto court and shared a few rallies with Ann.

For information and interest Ann Haydon-Jones was a powerful lawn tennis player. As Ann Haydon she won the 1954 and 1955 British Junior Championships. In 1956 she won the Wimbledon girls' Championship. Ann Haydon played tennis in a highly competitive era that included Billie Jean King, Margaret Court and Maria Bueno. She won the 1961 French Open Championship and reached the final of the 1961 U.S. Championships. In 1962 she married P.F.Jones and won the French Open for the second time. In 1967 at the Wimbledon and U.S. Championships, now Ann Haydon-Jones, reached the finals of both,

1992 Rosie Smythe on court with Anne Haydon-Jones.

Ann Haydon-Jones at Wimbledon.

2008 The last photograph of Rosie Smythe taken at the Marston Green Lawn Tennis Club with Ladies Singles Finalists Debbie Seazall and Carol Hunt.

2009 Mixed Doubles match on main court. Marston Green players at far end, Rory Lynas and partner Debbie Seazell.

but lost them to Billie Jean King. Two years later, the pair met again in the Wimbledon final, but this time Ann Haydon-Jones took the most coveted trophy in the sport, making her the first left handed female to do so.

She capped that year's Wimbledon victory by winning the Mixed Doubles Championship with Australian Fred Stolle. That same year was made even more memorable for her when she was voted as the B.B.C. Sports Personality of the Year.

2007 Open Mixed Doubles Winners Rory Lynas and Debbie Seazell on the left with Runners Up Lewis and Paige Willis on the right.

Improvements to the Clubhouse mentioned earlier, involved removing the rear section of the old wooden building, and laying out enlarged changing rooms, kitchen area and bar all within a new brick built extension.

Marston Green L.T.C. are proud of being known as a family club and do encourage youngsters to play as much tennis as possible. Parents play a big part in this and because they are at the Club so often, some do end up playing themselves. The Club membership at the present time is 55 Senior members and 25 Intermediates.

2009 Arrangement of the new brick section interfacing with the 1923 timber original.

Layout of the courts relative to the Clubhouse taken from the far end. Marston Green has four Synthetic Grass courts of which two are floodlit and one Macadam court which is also floodlit. League matches are played on the Synthetic Grass. The Macadam court is to replaced by Synthetic Grass at a later date in the next few years.

BOWLS:

Marston Green Crown Green Bowling Club was formed in January 1991 and they utilized ground at the rear of St.Leonard's Church in Elmdon Road to lay out their crown green. A committee was formed and membership offered to Gentlemen and Ladies who wished to take part in crown green bowling. The Club plays in a local league, plays internal competitions and has friendly matches against other clubs.

1991 An early photograph taken alongside the new green. Approximately 40 local villagers turned up for an inaugural gathering of prospective members present. The current membership which is fairly constant numbers about 70 and the Club are always pleased to welcome potential members.

Club members in general play on the Crown Green.

The same year in September following the enthusiasm and enjoyment by the members it was agreed to form a 'short mat' section for the winter months. The regular days for short mat are Tuesday and Wednesday afternoons and matches are played in the Parish Hall. Four mats are used, drawn at random, and at the present time the Club run 4 teams in League bowling during the winter months. The Club have been successful in both formats of bowling, the crown green team were winners of Division V in 2002 and the short mat team won the Championship of Division IV.

2002 Winners of Division V of the 'Over 60s' Crown Green League. Front row: Brian Pace, Dennis Bishop, Jack Rawlins and Maurice Raybould. At rear: John Halden and Ron Wilson.

Winners of Division IV – Short Mat League. Rear row: Derek Wilson, Ron Wilson, John Halden and Tom Dick. Centre: Peggy Martin, Jack Rawlins, Margaret Halden and Dorothy Wilson. Front: Kay Sumner, Roger Underwood and Audrey Laight.

Chapter 27

MARSTON GREEN IN WARTIME

IN THE early days of the 1939/45 War there was a considerable amount of activity in the village. Trenches were dug at numerous points around the village fields, we were informed that this was done to disrupt random landing of gliders and aircraft. Many householders had holes dug in their gardens ready for the installation of corrugated iron 'Anderson' Air Raid Shelters. Some shops piled sandbags in front of their premises to minimise effects of damage likely to be caused by bombing.

Villagers were organised to form various emergency organisations, such as A.R.P. (Air Raid Precautions), later changing its name to 'Civil Defence'. A.F.S. (Auxiliary Fire Service) and 'The Home Guard'. The old St.Leonard's Church at the corner of Land Lane and Station Road was turned into a First Aid Post and a fabricated Fire Station was erected on what is now known as the Memorial Garden.

'Chapel House Farm' in Elmdon Lane which is now the Station Car Park became the headquarters of the 'Home Guard'. In those early days, these various organisations carried out 'dummy runs' exercises to gain experience of what would be required of them if enemy activities came to Marston Green.

Large numbers of young men and women were called up into the Armed Forces, some sadly never to return. The brass plaques mounted later in the Memorial Garden list those unfortunate villagers from both world wars who gave their lives in the fight against enemy aggression. Quite ironically, there were 13 villagers lost in both wars.

WORLD WAR I 1914/1918		WORLD WAR II 1939/1945	
J.AUSTIN	G.SMITH	W.H.ASHMORE	L.A.A.SMITH
P.BROMFIELD	J.SMITH	N.G.BOWKER	R.A.STEVENS
H.FARROW	R.TIMMINS	J.GALLAHAR	R.WATERS
R.GILSON	L.WILSON	L.GREGORY	S.WILLIAMSON
T.HOLMES		G.H.HILL	
F.MELLISH		D.HUDDLESTON	
A.MITCHELL		N.W.LEWIS	
A.NEWELL		S.MOORE	
H.SIMPSON		D.ONIONS	

Towards the end of 1940, Marston Green felt the effects of the war more than hitherto and there were many night air raids which kept the A.R.P. and A.F.S. contingents continually on the alert. Marston Green had its fair share of bombs actually dropping in the immediate environs, but fortunately very little structural damage was caused to property in the village.

The first bomb that fell landed in Wood Lane (now leading to Moor End Avenue), but very, very fortunately in this case it did not explode. My father Edmund Crawford and Frank Alcott were the first A.R.P. Personnel on the scene, they roped off the area and sent for the 'professionals' (Bomb Disposal) to defuse the bomb. Apparently when they returned to Wood Lane, a young Bill Harrow had climbed down into the hole to investigate.

As far as my memory recalls having listened to my father sending off reports, there were only three hits from bombs on property in Marston Green. 'Hall House' which stood behind the Free Church was severely damaged. The last bungalow on the right of Land Lane nearest to the Railway Bridge had some structural damage and was repaired fairly quickly. No.28 Holly Lane the home of Vic Riley and family was so badly damaged that it had to be demolished and rebuilt. The bomb which landed on the Riley house was the last one of a 'stick' of bombs which started in the fields past the Airport, crossed Elmdon Lane by Marston Green Station and finished in Holly Lane. One of the bombs burst a water main, which caused considerable inconvenience to the residents at the Station end of Elmdon Lane, and for several days they had to get their water from portable water 'bowsers', whilst 'standpipes' had to be used in other parts of the village.

A remarkable effect of the bomb on the Riley house was that although some houses on both sides of Holly Lane had windows broken, the large plate glass windows of my father's shop remained intact, despite the fact that the shop was virtually opposite the bombed building. At the time of the bomb landing, I was in our Air Raid Shelter with my mother and younger sister in the rear garden of the shop, when we heard a clattering noise above the shelter which was unexplained at the time. The next morning we found a rather battered dust bin from the Riley house on top of the shelter, having been blown right over the shop by the force of the blast.

I suppose it is fair to say that Marston Green was not a target for the German bombers and the majority of bombs that fell were intended for Elmdon Airport as it was then known. German bombers also followed the Coventry to Birmingham railway line as a positive route to Birmingham which of course did receive considerable bombing. It was about the same period that the Airport received a day time visit by German bombers. A 'Junkers 88' made a low level attack on the aerodrome, dropped three bombs, and carried on and machine gunned the village itself. Fortunately, there were no reported incidents of personal injuries.

There was a lull in bombing raids for some time, but the raids resumed again in 1941, with incendiary bombs being the main weapon. It is not recorded how many incendiaries were dropped because many of them landed on 'open land' and burned themselves out.

It was during these incendiary raids that 'Hall House' was hit by a bomb and several properties were hit by incendiaries. Due to the vigilance of various groups operating in the village, damage was superficial, and in the majority of cases, was confined to the roof areas of the properties and quickly dealt with.

One of the largest bombs that was dropped in the vicinity of the village was a 'Land Mine' which drifted towards the village suspended by a parachute. Good fortune prevailed, and the bomb landed in a tree in the area scheduled to be the golf course later with its striker just a few feet from the ground.

At the Marston Green Station there used to be a steel framed footbridge, which crossed the lines from Holly Lane to the Birmingham platform. The horizontal walkway across the lines comprised a deep steel girder with a wide flange at the top. When bombing occurred over Birmingham or Coventry, the bridge became a vantage point for witnessing the raids. Observers to the bombing used to scratch lines in the direction of the explosions and later were able to identify the actual location of the recipients of the bombing.

After a while through scrutiny of the scratched lines, it was possible to identify which factories were being attacked – 'Courtaulds', 'Massey Ferguson', 'G.E.C.', 'Alvis' 'B.T.H.' at Coventry and 'Dunlop', 'B.S.A.', 'Lucas', 'Metropolitan Cammell', 'Guest Keen and Nettlefold', and 'I.C.I.' at Birmingham being amongst regular targets during the worst of the bombing. A direct hit on the bridge would certainly have resulted in a lot of mourning families in the village.

From records taken at the time it was calculated that some 500 bombs of all types actually fell around the village and the immediate surroundings, but the majority fell on open ground.

As the war progressed, Elmdon Airport was used for early training of 'R.A.F.' and 'Fleet Air Arm' pilots and the 'Tiger Moth' was the light aircraft used for this purpose. 'Stirling' bombers were assembled at the 'shadow' factory built for 'Short's' at Elmdon' and flown to the war zones. Before the war there used to be what was called the 'Tin Hospital' located about a mile past the houses in Elmdon Lane. It was built after the First World War for treatment of servicemen who had been gassed in the trenches but remained as an 'Isolation Hospital' for many years. When the 'shadow factory' was built it was demolished to enable a wide bridge to be built to facilitate the towing of 'Stirling' bombers from the factory to the Airport. The footings of the bridge can still be seen on the way to Coventry by train.

A military hospital was built in Berwicks Lane for wounded Canadian servicemen, and this hospital was retained after the war and became 'Marston Green Maternity Hospital'. It remained as a favoured maternity unit, certainly for locals and remained for the best part of 40 years. The site has now been built on and the main road through the area is logically called Maple Leaf Drive.

The frequency of Air Raids which actually affected the village, diminished such that the final months of the war passed quietly in Marston Green. One noticeable feature of the war could be seen around the local farms and most of them employed 'Land Army Girls', a civilian army of volunteers girls who took over to replace the many farming workers who had joined the armed forces. Around the area several Prisoner of War Camps were located, Packington and Maxstoke Park were two of the largest and many smaller ones were also established.

The prisoners were mainly Italian, they worked on the farms, they did essential road repairs, dug ditches and carried out other similar activities, and at times they would be seen carrying out their duties, apparently unsupervised in the village. Towards the end of the war Germans came along.

One young 17 year old German Prisoner named Walter Roske arrived at Maxstoke in October 1944 and worked on a couple of farms in Marston Green. In his spare time in the Camp he made toys, aeroplanes, chess figures and rope slippers. He tried to sell them outside the camp and on one occasion he met Mrs. Hardman, the mother of Margaret (Cuthbertson), Dorothy (Harvey), Gwen and Barbara. She invited him to make 4 pairs of slippers for her daughters. The Italians were allowed to return home within weeks of the war ending but the Germans including Walter Roske were kept here until early in 1948.

In those years he often saw the Hardman family, and one year they invited him to spend Christmas with them and because of their generosity and kindness he kept in touch with Barbara when he returned to Germany. He had helped her as she had been taking German at school whilst he was here. In 1990, she invited him and his wife Herta to come to Blackpool, to her 30th Wedding Anniversary.

They brought him to Marston Green and George and Margaret Cuthbertson took them both to Maxstoke. Knowing of this friendship I wrote to him in 1997 as I was writing the 100th Anniversary Book of Maxstoke Park Golf Club. He replied and indicated that when he stood at the Golf Club driveway which had been the entrance to the Prison of War Camp where he had spent 4 years of his life and seeing everything looking so peaceful at that moment he admitted he shed a few tears.

There were something like 50 members of the A.R.P. spread around the village, they were sectionalised, with each group having a particular area for

1944 Walter Roske at Maxstoke.

1940 to 1945 The A.F.S. (Auxiliary Fire Service) Brigade

Standing: Harry Mellish, Charles Moseley and Joe Martin. Seated: Jack Hamar, Oswald Richards,
George Kay, George Foster and Sid Tipper.

Standing: George Foster, Eric Mullis, Unknown, Dick Taylor, John Harrow, Harry Musson, Albert
Simmonds, Peter Roberts and George Roberts. Squatting: Wilfred Webb, Harry Hill, Harry Mellish, Jack
Hamar and Joe Martin. The Fire Station which was a pre-fabricated steel structured building and was
located on what is now the Memorial Garden. All of the Brigade members were 'volunteers' and most of
them had full time 'day time' jobs. They gave active cover at all times.

1940 A.R.P. (Air Raid Precautions) later Civil Defence in 1942

Rear Row: Walley, Henry Heath, Unknown., Levi Austin, Arthur Deeley and Troy 2nd Row: John Gardner, George Norman; Peddler, George Elvin-Morrison, Breakwell, Unknown, Unknown and Les Challenor. 3rd Row: John Heath, Arthur Harwood, Rev. Buckley, Ward, Unknown, Norman Wilson and Unknown. Front Row: Jolley, Unknown, Harold Bott, Roger Ward, Ernest Clare, Wilfred Martin and Elliott.

which they were responsible. To improve their 'skills' to enable them, hopefully, to control any problems that they would be likely to meet following an Air Raid, regular exercises were carried out to ensure that they were adequately trained in all aspects of rescue and emergency actions appropriate, as circumstances deemed necessary.

1942 A team from the Cook's Lane end of the village won an all 'Warwickshire Proficiency Competition' based upon the duties of Air Raid Wardens. That area did

1940 A typical training exercise to familiarise themselves with different aptitudes required for all aspects of victim recovery.

Marston Green Civil Defence Contingent Winners of the Warwickshire County Cup. Back Row: Bill Knibbs, Eddie Crawford, Joe Martin, Malcolm Keen, George Hill and Frank Medlicott. Centre Row: Ernie Belcher, Harry Vaughan, W.J.Mason (Head of Warwickshire Civil Defence), Frank Allcott, Nancy Hobson and Bill Ashmore. Front Row: Jack Hamar, Fred Priestley and Arthur Hall.

The Home Guard (Dad's Army). Photograph taken outside their Chapel House Farm Headquarters. From left to right: Back Row: 1. Jack Griffin, 2.Bill Bryant. 2nd Row: 1. Frank Riley, 7. Tony Cooper, 11. Bill Learner, 14. Arthur Morrison. 3rd Row: 1. George Andrews, 2. Eric Brelsford, 5. Mr Cotton, 7. Jack Rose, 8. Frank Smith, 9. Ken Phillips, 10. Mr Lilley, 11. Norman Wallace, 13. Len Martin. Front Row: 1. Les Thompson, 2. Jean Onions, 3. Ray Jester, 5. Clarrie Robinson, 7. Frank Swindell, 8. Pat Yarnell, 9. Frank Robinson, 10. Sgt.Major Wilson, 14. Bert Onions.

not have a messenger and they asked the Marston Green Wardens if they could borrow one of the messengers that were available in the village. I agreed to ride for them as my father was a friend of George Hill, the local postman and who was the leader of their team. It was lucky for we won, and I was fortunate enough to be in the right place at the right time, and was duly presented with a winner's certificate. My father was in a Marston Green team that won later on to keep it in the family.

For some years after the war finished, the 'Civil Defence' carried on, this was due to the 'strained cold war' that existed between Russia and the West for some time.

The 'Special' Constabulary

Standing: 1. Fred Gosbell, 2. Ted Myers, 3. Les Sharrad, 6. Les Thompson, 7. S.Jefferies. Seated: 1. Sam Rawlins, 2. Harry Anderton, 3. Bert Perkins, 4. Police Constable Russell, 5. Reg Aston.

HEART OF ENGLAND AIR TRAINING CORPS
Taken at 'Syreston' R.A.F. Bomber Squadron, near Nottingham 1942

Taken at 'Syreston' R.A.F. Bomber Squadron, near Nottingham 1942. Rear Row: 3. Harvey Antrobus, 5. Graham Crawford, 9. John Underhill. Second Row: 2. Chris McLaren, 9. Dick Miller. Third Row: 1. Ted Brayshay, 6. Rod McLaren, 7. Tom Hayward. Front Row: 5. Brian Jackson, 9. Raymond Walker.

Efficiency competitions were held at regular intervals based upon a 'County Championship' format to keep the members up to date with latest techniques.

On the night of the visit everyone was given a 'worm's eye view' at the end of the runway to watch a squadron of 'Lancaster' bombers taking off for raids on Germany. As the bombers were coming towards us we were all sitting on the grass at the boundary fence. As they came closer, we all slid down and by the time they cleared the fence, we were all lying flat out – horizontal. At dawn the next morning, a return was made to the same vantage point to watch them return – three of them didn't, but memory says, one damaged plane landed safely somewhere in Norfolk.

Chapter 28

NEW HOUSING 1990-2010

ALONG ELMDON Road, opposite the roadway to Aylesford Drive leading off the approach to the railway bridge, a cluster of houses were built starting in 1994. The approach roadway off Elmdon Road is Somerton Drive leading on to Wolverton Road, which branches off on the left to Rotherby Grove, and continues on to Farndon Avenue. The houses are of attractive design, varied, with 5 and 4 bed-roomed detached houses, and good sized semi-detached properties all of a high standard.

2009 Houses Nos.2 to 8 in Somerton Drive with Elmdon Road to the right.

2009 To the left off Somerton Drive, houses No.2 to 10 in Wolverton Road.

From the previous photograph, it can be seen that Wolverton Road carries on for some 120 yards down a slight incline, branching off at the bend to Farndon Avenue on the right, the road sign at the bottom indicated Rotherby Grove to the left.

2009 No.5 Farndon Avenue at the junction with Wolverton Road. Road sign indicates Nos.2 to 8 to the left, Nos.7 to 11 and Nos.16 and 18 to the right.

2009 Farndon Avenue to the left of the photograph above. The houses pictured are in a row of 4, numbered No.2 far right to No.8 on the left.

2009 Wolverton Road and Rotherby Grove junction. Looking back to houses in Somerton Drive off Elmdon Road.

2009 Three terraced apartments in Rotherby Grove Nos.10 to 12 with six detached properties No.3 and 5 to 9 inclusive further back at rear.

2009 At the same junction in Rotherby Grove Nos.15 to 18 off to the right. Houses past the taller building on the right and beyond the low hedge are in Hidcote Grove.

After 'Chelmsley Hospital' was closed towards the late 1990s, an extensive planning application was submitted to build a new housing complex on most of the old hospital site and associated grounds. There were objections raised in the early stages against the number of houses submitted which were considered to be excessive.

Eventually a proposal for some 300 houses was accepted and building commenced in the early 2000s and took some 5 years for final completion of the project.

As an appreciation of the historic and significant contribution that the Canadian Military Hospital brought to the village during the war years, the main thoroughfare in the new housing was called Maple Leaf Drive. This roadway started in Berwicks Lane at the far corner of 'Chelmsley Town' football pitch.

2009 The 'John Black Day Hospital' off Maple Leaf Drive.

Maple Leaf Drive wound its way more or less past where the hospital had been situated and continued on with several twists and turns through the estate. Eventually finishing where the old hospital boundary nearest to the village had been, making a junction with an entrance roadway named Brookland's Way which came off a new roundabout in Coleshill Road below 'Pinewood Business Park'.

These new buildings are positioned at the far side of the Chelmsley Town Football Club pitch and is more or less where the original Canadian Hospital was located.

I am not sure what the significance of this building is. When the Canadian Hospital was there during the war, the roadway which now leads to the football ground extended further along, past a bungalow which later was the residence of

2009 The 'Gatehouse' and commemorative brickwork in Maple Leaf Drive.

2009 Maple Leaf Drive at the junction with Brooklands Way.

Mrs. Maxwell the Matron of the Maternity Hospital, and would have reached this location. Had there been at that time, another building called the 'Gatehouse' which would have been the official entrance to the Canadian Hospital?

'Chelmsley Farm' as mentioned earlier, was probably more that 200 years old, and at times had different names due to change of ownership. In 1878 when the 'Cottage Homes' were built, the farm was taken over and continued as a working farm but from then on the dairy produce, all manner of vegetables, meat from their own herds and poultry went to ensure that the 'Cottage Homes' were self sufficient. By the 1990s due to the running down of 'Chelmsley Hospital', as it was then called, the farm was no longer needed and the barns and other outbuildings fell into disrepair. Whilst the new 'Wavers Marston' complex was being built, these buildings were refurbished and converted into two bedroomed terraced cottages.

2009 The well designed layout of the converted barns which have been incorporated into the 'Wavers Marston' complex.

2009 'Wavers Marston' properties viewed through the security fence from the footpath leading into Marston Green Park from Chelmsley Lane. The buildings to the left are the rear of the terraced cottages following the barn conversions.

2009 The rear of the converted barns from Chelmsley Farm looking towards the security fence in the picture above. The access gateway through to the Marston Green Park is permanently locked, but those living in the converted barns and the houses opposite, were allocated a key. The houses opposite where the cars can be seen, are numbered 107 to 121.

2009 Converted barn cottages shown are Nos.129 and 133 to 139. The other cottages beyond these cottages are numbered 123 to 127 whilst the cottage on the right of the photograph with wooden fence is No. 131. When the barns were converted, the cottages were sold only to people aged over 55. This section of roadway in Wavers Marston is the only one indicating that it is a Private Road.

2009 Individual houses taken further along the boundary fence to the footpath in Marston Green Park. Both of these larger properties have as can be seen, have double garages. The gate gives access from Wagstaff Way.

'Wavers Marston' rather strangely does not refer to a locality, but in this case it is the main road through the housing complex. Off Moor End Avenue, it travels a short distance to the buildings seen below and swings away to the right. Again after a short distance the road turns to the left, turns left again at the next corner, then running parallel with the boundary fence of Marston Green Park it passes Wagstaff Way, Clarksland Grove and a small cul de sac on the right, turns left again and returns on its circuitous route to the junction of the apartments on the photograph.

2009 Large apartment blocks as you enter 'Wavers Marston' off Moor End Avenue.

2009 Typical mix of houses which applies to most of 'Wavers Marston' roads.

2009 Clarksland Grove leading down to Marston Green Park.

2009 Access gateway from Clarksland Grove to Marston Green Park. The fence is the boundary of 'Wavers Marston' where it runs from No. 64 Chelmsley Lane, the house seen past the new dwellings on the photograph.

2009 'Wavers Marston' houses adjacent to Wood Lane.

2009 No.64 Chelmsley Lane with the new 'Wavers Marston' houses beyond.

In recent years Marston Green has been a target for property developers, not all have been successful, but Coleshill Road seemed to be a main attraction, where many properties had large rear gardens. The first of these was a 'Wimpey' project which they called 'The Willows'. An elderly lady lived on her own in an old bungalow at No.64 and when very good friends of hers decided to move to 'Seaton' in Devon, knowing that she had no living relative, they invited her to go with them. Her bungalow therefore was put up for sale by her friends, and amongst other potential developers, 'Wimpey' spoke to neighbours and made promises to give more than the market price to build in their gardens. An initial planning application was submitted to knock five properties down and replace them with ten 4 bedroomed houses. There was tremendous opposition to this by the Parish Council, the local Residents Association and by many close neighbours in Coleshill Road and the application was turned down by the Solihull Planning Department.

A second submission was submitted by 'Wimpey' but in their favour, due to the considerable opposition with respect to knocking 5 houses down they withdrew that application. Finally, they agreed to an acceptable compromise of simply demolishing the bungalow to make an access road to the rear gardens, and build just 6 'dormer' bungalows and 4 detached houses. This submission was passed and building started in June 2005.

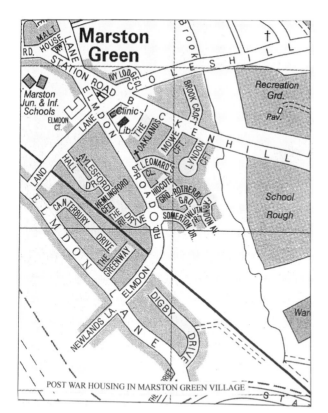

Post War Housing in Marston Green Village

2007 The access from Coleshill Road leading to two of the 'dormer' bungalows which were positioned in the gardens of No.60 and 62 and 62a. The developers agreed to retain most of the mature trees on the site, and the tree shown within the shrubbery was one in the boundary hedge between No.62 and the demolished bungalow.

2007 Four more 'dormer' bungalows to the right at the end of the access drive. Three of the bungalows to the left are in the rear garden of No.62, the one facing on the right backs into the garden of No.60. The retained tree to the left is a 'scotch pine'.

2007 Two of the 4 bedroomed houses which back on to the Recreation Ground with the boundary hedge visible between the houses.

2007 The largest of the detached houses which is positioned alongside the access drive facing Coleshill Road in line with the frontages of the existing buildings in the road. Whilst 'Wimpey' referred to the site as 'The Willows' the properties were later given a name with local connotation as Musson Close. The 'Musson' family were farmers of long standing of some 100 years in the village, started by W.J.Musson and continued by his 2 sons, John at 'Chelmsley Farm' and Harry at 'Gorse Farm'.

As an indication as to the area involved in the site, the rear gardens of the existing properties was some 75 yards. The new rear garden of No.62 is more or less 25 yards to the new fence. The Oak trees in the front garden were probably there before the property, old Survey Maps show Coleshill Road as tree lined without houses evident.

Further along Coleshill Road are two other developments. One which is near to completion has already been named as Merstone Close. This development involved modernising and enlarging two 4 bedroomed existing properties Nos.84 and 86, and adding three new 4 bedroomed houses in the gardens.

2009 Merstone Close Coleshill Road comprising five 4 bedroomed houses. The other development which at the present moment is called 'The Hollies' involves the demolition of No.94 and replacing it with 7 houses of different sizes of 3, 4 and 5 bedrooms.

2009 The 'Hollies' in Coleshill Road under construction.

Across the road there used to be a 4 bedroomed bungalow numbered No.47 Coleshill Road. A planning application was approved to demolish this bungalow and replace it with two new properties. Unfortunately, this was done midway through 2008, the demolition took place, the financial recession came along and halted the project. The site has been fenced off and, at the time of going to print, there was no sign of any progress.

2008 No.47 Coleshill Road.

2009 The fenced off area where the original bungalow was positioned.

Chapter 29

MEMORIES OF CHELMSLEY WOODS

BRIDGES ANCIENT AND MODERN

An early bridge probably taken early 1900s crossing 'Low Brook' with the rough track continuing to the entrance to 'Alcott Woods'. The wooden fence running past on the right was the original boundary fence of the 'Cottage Homes'.

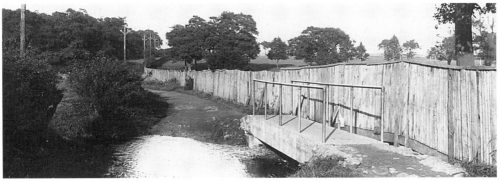

This is the bridge that was there pre war.

2009 A pedestrian only bridge from Wood Lane adjacent to Moor End Avenue.

ALCOTT WOODS

1925 The Gate and Stile about 100 yards past the old bridges, which was the entry into 'Alcott Woods'. The gate was positioned to the left of present day Moor End Avenue more or less where the remaining trees still stand. The old track as can be seen, continued on a winding 'zig zag' route for some 300 to 400 yards eventually straightening where Berwicks Lane today meets Moor End Avenue and arrived at the old 'Alcott Hall Farm' which in those days was a large working farm, and can be seen on page 20.

1925 The winding track through 'Alcott Wood' which carried on to 'Alcott Hall'.

1925 A typical scene in 'Chelmsley Woods'. The trees were predominantly 'Oaks', 'Birch', 'Mountain Ash', 'Sycamores', 'Poplars' and scattered 'conifers'.

1925 Taken on the raised pathway through 'Chelmsley Woods'. The pathway was referred to as Bridge Road on old Ordnance Survey Maps. The entrance to the woods was by way of a stile, about 100 yards across a planted field immediately past 'Alcott Hall Farm', roughly where 'Pine Square' is located today.

The pathway through the Woods continued for about 1¼ miles until it reached the Chester Road (A446). Crossing the road you could continue to Coleshill by way of Green Lane which was the preferred route by bicycle in the summer months for those of us who went to school in Coleshill in those days. No school buses in those days, and the Marston Green to Coleshill bus route only ran every two hours, not very convenient times sadly.